ENCOUNTERS WITH JESUS

ENCOUNTERS WITH JESUS

Ben Witherington III

CASCADE *Books* • Eugene, Oregon

ENCOUNTERS WITH JESUS

Cascade Books
An Imprint of Wipf and Stock Publishers
199 W. 8th Ave., Suite 3
Eugene, OR 97401

www.wipfandstock.com

PAPERBACK ISBN: 978-1-5326-9825-5
HARDCOVER ISBN: 978-1-5326-9826-2
EBOOK ISBN: 978-1-5326-9827-9

Cataloguing-in-Publication data:

Names: Witherington III, Ben
Title: Encounters with Jesus / Ben Witherington III.
Description: Eugene, OR: Cascade Books, 2020
Identifiers: ISBN 978-1-5326-9825-5 (paperback) | ISBN 978-1-5326-9826-2 (hardcover) | ISBN 978-1-5326-9827-9 (ebook)
Subjects: LCSH: Jesus Christ—Biography | Bible stories—New Testament
Classification: BT302 W58 2020 (print) | BT302 (ebook)

Manufactured in the U.S.A.   AUGUST 18, 2020

This study is dedicated to two of my former NT doctoral students who now have their PhDs—Judith Odor and Joy Vaughan. May the women in half of these vignettes inspire your ongoing ministry.

And for Mimi Haddad. Thanks for all your wonderful hard work for the CBE and for your unfailing support for women in ministry.

BW3

CONTENTS

PREFACE

THE GOSPELS ARE EPISODIC ACCOUNTS OF THE LIFE OF JESUS, BY WHICH I mean they are necessarily very selective in their presentation of Jesus' life and work. We could have deduced this easily enough from the remark at the end of the Fourth Gospel which states "Jesus did many other things as well. If every one of them were written down, I suppose even the whole world would not have room for the books that would be written" (John 21:25). This book is not an attempt to tell or imagine more stories from the life of Jesus (on which see my *The Gospel of Jesus*), but rather to fill in some of the gaps in the stories that we do have in the canonical Gospels. In particular, this book is an attempt to let those whom Jesus touched, healed, helped, tell their own stories while drawing on the Gospel accounts verbatim.

Let me be clear that what is going on here is historical reconstruction, not flights of fancy, or the turning of Jesus' life into pulp fiction. Based on what can be known about the context in which these events happened (the historical, social, archaeological, religious contexts), I have sought to give a dramatic presentation of what it might have been like to talk with those Jesus touched, and get their reaction to the miracles and happenings that changed their lives. I am not attempting to add to, or subtract from, what we have in the Scriptures, but rather to creatively present a broader canvas, a wider framework in which to better understand the Scriptural texts. Yes, this involves some creativity, but not creativity for its own sake. If this helps these stories come to light in fresh ways, I am content. I have generally quoted the Gospels from the NIV with small variations where I thought they made mistakes. I thank Stan Gundry and Zondervan for permission to use the old NIV in this little novella. The Scriptures portions are in italics, but without including verses in the text so you will read these narratives as they were originally heard—as continuous stories.

One more thing. I have chosen to use a few more original forms of various of the important names in these stories, so you can get a feel for how these people were originally named and called in Jesus' own day. Here's a short list:

Jesus=Yeshua=Joshua
Mary=Miriam
James=Jacob
Lazarus=Eliezar
God=G-d (Jews avoided saying God's name due to reverence)

A few place names as well are modified to be more like the original for example Migdal is the town of Mary Magdalene, so she's really Miriam of Migdal.

Christmas 2019

CHAPTER ONE

JOHN THE BAPTIZER

"I REMEMBER THAT THE HEAT WAS SEVERE, BUT BY THEN MY DISCIPLES had gotten used to it. I, for my part, spent so much time in the desert and in the Jordan that it didn't much bother me. Besides, my time in the Essene community by the Salt Sea had hardened me when it comes to heat. When people asked why the Essenes had so many mikvehs[1] and water rituals, I just laughed. When you are living in the salt flats, all you think about is water to sooth your fevered brow. That saying from Isaiah was our theme— "a voice crying: in the wilderness make straight a highway for our G-d." The Essenes interpreted that to mean that they needed to prepare by the Salt Sea, the Judean chalk wilderness. Eventually, I had other ideas, but there was no denying their sincerity. They were right that G-d was about to intervene, but even I could not have imagined how that would transpire.

---

1. This is a ritual purification pool used to remove various sorts of uncleanness.

1

"Yes, my mother told me the story about Miriam, the much younger cousin of my mother. The story of a miraculous conception was not hard to believe, in light of what happened to Elizabeth, my mother, who had an experience much like Sarah, long ago. But a virgin conceiving, and without the aid of a husband, well that was too much for some people. Nobody had read Isaiah that way before then. The text said this—

"Then Isaiah said, 'Hear now, you house of David! Is it not enough to try the patience of humans? Will you try the patience of my G-d also? Therefore the Lord himself will give you a sign: The virgin will conceive and give birth to a son, and will call him Immanuel. He will be eating curds and honey when he knows enough to reject the wrong and choose the right, for before the boy knows enough to reject the wrong and choose the right, the land of the two kings you dread will be laid waste. The Lord will bring on you and on your people and on the house of your father a time unlike any since Ephraim broke away from Judah—he will bring the king of Assyria.'

"We had all understood this to refer to an event during the time of Isaiah in light of the latter part of that passage. We also had understood it to mean that a nubile woman who had remained a virgin until marriage would conceive in the normal way, with aid of her new husband, and give birth to a worthy royal heir. As for Immanuel, we took that as a throne name, a title of sorts 'G-d with us' not a personal name, and certainly not a description of his nature.

"Of course, as I have learned over many years, the old prophecies have a way of coming true partially in olden times, but more fully now that the divine saving activity of G-d is at hand, the final intervention to save G-d's people. But what would that final intervention look like? What form would it take? The prophecies have depth and complexity to them and can be interpreted in various ways. What I came to be convinced of was that the intervention was imminent, and that I needed to be the harbinger of it, I needed to be the 'voice' crying in a more direct way than the Essenes. After all, no one could hear the Essenes if they announced the coming Dominion of G-d by the Salt Sea except other members of the community! This seemed to me not what Isaiah was calling for. I felt the need to leave that community and go confront Israel directly, so I conceived a plan to accomplish this mission.

"I would go to the Jordan, near the King's highway, and even better near the crossroads where the east-west road met the King's highway. This way I would encounter many Jews, and indeed even non-Jews on their way to the north or south, or Jericho or Jerusalem, or in the other direction towards Nabatea and Petra.

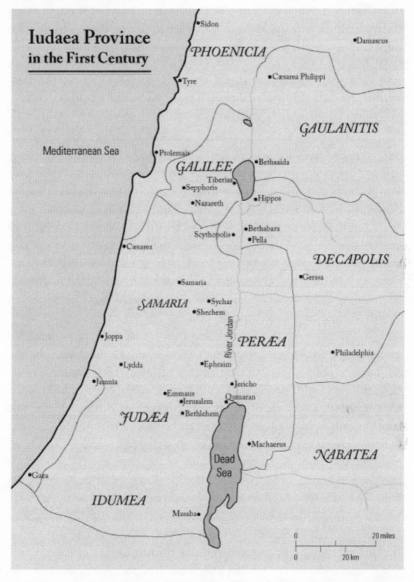

Iudaea Province in the First Century

"My message was much the same as the Essenes—'repent for the divine intervention judging G-d's people is at hand'. We all believed on the basis of the Scriptures that 'judgment begins with the household of G-d'. I agreed with the Essenes that the Herodian clan was hopelessly corrupt,

3

and the priesthood tainted as well. I had no interest in attending festivals in Herod's temple. In my view it was doomed from the start. But the rest of my family did not necessarily agree. However, I had little contact with them after I came of age. I was off to the Salt Sea by then. Exactly what form G-d's judgment on his sinful people would take, I was not sure. Sometimes I thought 'the Coming One' would be G-d himself, but sometimes I thought it might be a messianic figure who would judge the Twelve tribes. The prophecies were clear about judgment coming, but not about whether it would be direct divine judgment or not.

"In any case, what was very clear is that it would not be 'good news' but rather bad news for Israel, unless of course Israel repented. I certainly had not expected it would come through my cousin Yeshua, and I still have my questions, though I doubt now I will get answers. My time is almost at hand. As I sit here rotting in Antipas's cell in the Machereus awaiting my fate, I am still hoping to hear from my disciples who have gone to inquire of Yeshua. I am thankful that at least one member of Herod's entourage, this woman named Joanna, the wife of Chuza, has come and is taking down my story. At least some will know what has happened to me. But let us go back to that most remarkable of days, now almost a year ago—the day when Yeshua himself came to be baptized by me.

"Let me first say that I had heard the rumors and stories about his performing miracles and announcing 'good news.' Heard them, and had no reason to doubt them, but they clouded the picture in my mind of what G-d's will was for his people at this juncture. I, on the one hand, abstained from luxurious foods, did not mingle with notorious sinners, had only the animal skins on my back for clothing, and continually warned of coming judgment, prepared for by a baptism symbolizing repentance.

"Yeshua, from all reports, did almost the opposite. He announced coming good news, healed people, ate with sinners, and in general got a reputation as a drinker of wine and a friend of people who were not pious, were not Torah true. It was very puzzling, even strange. What was I supposed to think about all that? Had I been wrong about coming judgment on the land, on the temple, on the Herods, on the people?

"People had said I was like Elijah, but I performed no miracles like him. 'Elijah' they said, 'the one who comes before the great and terrible Day of the Lord'. I suppose my attire, and my message led to this idea, but Elijah was not a baptizer, and I did not go to the courts of Herod and speak truth to power directly like Elijah did. Yet they came to me and heard my message. I suppose I was seen as a threat—offering forgiveness without having to go to the priests in the temple and offer a sacrifice to receive pardon for sin. Had all the people come to me at the Jordan, they might not have felt a need to go to the temple for the purposes of repentance of sin.

"But I digress. Let's focus on 'that day' that Yeshua came to me. Joanna here can read you the version of the story she has just read to me, written down by Matthew, the tax collector . . ."

Joanna reads, *"In those days John the Baptist came, preaching in the wilderness of Judea and saying, 'Repent, for the kingdom of heaven has come near.' This is he who was spoken of through the prophet Isaiah:*

'A voice of one calling in the wilderness,
"Prepare the way for the Lord,
make straight paths for him."'

"John's clothes were made of camel's hair, and he had a leather belt around his waist. His food was locusts and wild honey. People went out to him from Jerusalem and all Judea and the whole region of the Jordan. Confessing their sins, they were baptized by him in the Jordan River.

"But when he saw many of the Pharisees and Sadducees coming to where he was baptizing, he said to them: 'You brood of vipers! Who warned you to flee from the coming wrath? Produce fruit in keeping with repentance. And do not think you can say to yourselves, "We have Abraham as our father." I tell you that out of these stones G-d can raise up children for Abraham. The ax is already at the root of the trees, and every tree that does not produce good fruit will be cut down and thrown into the fire.

'I baptize you with water for repentance. But after me comes one who is more powerful than I, whose sandals I am not worthy to carry. He will baptize you with the Holy Spirit and fire. His winnowing fork is in his hand, and he will clear his threshing floor, gathering his wheat into the barn and burning up the chaff with unquenchable fire.'

"Then Yeshua came from Galilee to the Jordan to be baptized by John. But John tried to deter him, saying, 'I need to be baptized by you, and do you come to me?'

"Yeshua replied, 'Let it be so now; it is proper for us to do this to fulfill all righteousness.' Then John consented.

"As soon as Yeshua was baptized, he went up out of the water. At that moment heaven was opened, and he saw the Spirit of G-d descending like a dove and alighting on him. And a voice from heaven said, 'This is my Son, whom I love; with him I am well pleased.' [Matthew 3]

After Joanna reads, John continues, "It was at that juncture, that I said 'Behold the Lamb of G-d, who takes away the sins of the world'. If you have any communication with G-d at all you realize there are moments of insight, bursts of clear thinking when a truth comes through to you that previously you had not even imagined. Sometimes we say more than we currently know or understand, and that was one of those times, I suppose. Yet as I sit here now, awaiting the return of my disciples, or my fate, which-ever comes more quickly, I still have questions about whether Yeshua is 'the One who is to Come'. I also wonder if my ministry did more than just get my followers in trouble with the Herodian authorities, whose spies are everywhere. What did I really accomplish? Many came and were baptized, and many seemed sincere in their repentance, but what will happen now? Who can say? Yeshua apparently once called me the greatest of the prophets of the old era, indeed the greatest man ever conceived and born the normal way of woman. What would he say of me now—skin and bones, chained in a dank cell, awaiting execution?"

At this juncture, one of John's disciples shows up at the Machereus and gives the following report: "Master, we have caught up with Yeshua, and here is his reply to your questions. I have taken time to memorize it verbatim, noting it alludes to the prophecies of Isaiah. He said 'Go and report to John what you hear and see: the blind receive sight, and the lame walk, the lepers are cleansed and the deaf hear, the dead are raised up, and the poor have the gospel preached to them.' And blessed is he who does not take offense at Me." [Matthew 11]

John listened quietly to these words, and murmured—"So it is true. So there is to be a healing even with the repentance and judgment. But no man has ever given sight to the blind before Yeshua. There is no record of it in the Hebrew Scriptures, only a promise of it in Isaiah. So the stories are true—my cousin is 'the Coming One' but G-d's redemptive judgment is taking a form I never conceived of before now. Hallelujah, and so be it—Amen."

Joanna must continue the story from here. "It was at this juncture that the Herodian jailor came and took John. I was present to see the horrors that happened, being part of Herod's household because of my husband Chuza. I recorded the events as follows.

"Herod himself had given orders to have John arrested, and he had him bound and put in prison. He did this because of Herodias, his brother Philip's wife, whom he had married. For John had been saying to Herod, 'It is

not lawful for you to have your brother's wife.' So Herodias nursed a grudge against John and wanted to kill him. But she was not able to, because Herod feared John and protected him, knowing him to be a righteous and holy man. When Herod heard John, he was greatly puzzled; yet he liked to listen to him.

"Finally the opportune time came. On his birthday Herod gave a banquet for his high officials and military commanders and the leading men of Galilee. When the daughter of Herodias came in and danced, she pleased Herod and his dinner guests.

"The king said to the girl, 'Ask me for anything you want, and I'll give it to you.' And he promised her with an oath, 'Whatever you ask I will give you, up to half my kingdom.'

"She went out and said to her mother, 'What shall I ask for?'

"'The head of John the Baptizer,' she answered.

"At once the girl hurried in to the king with the request: 'I want you to give me right now the head of John the Baptizer on a platter.'

"The king was greatly distressed, but because of his oaths and his dinner guests, he did not want to refuse her. So he immediately sent an executioner with orders to bring John's head. The man went, beheaded John in the prison, and brought back his head on a platter. He presented it to the girl, and she gave it to her mother. On hearing of this, John's disciples came and took his body and laid it in a tomb. [Mark 6]

"I could say more about how John proved to be right when he said 'I must decrease, and he must increase' and yet it is also true that John continued to have disciples for many decades after his death [Acts 19]. At least in the end John had some peace about what his cousin was doing, some reassurance that his own ministry had not been for nothing. He prepared the way, but few could have guessed all that would come in the wake of the cry 'make straight a highway for our G-d.'"

CHAPTER TWO

THE WOMAN WITH THE FLOW OF BLOOD

DESPERATE. THAT'S THE ONLY WORD FOR IT. NONE OF THOSE PHYSICIANS had been any help at all. Well, there is a question whether they really know what they are doing when it comes to women's troubles anyway. Better to trust a healer. As I was saying, I was desperate. When you have a continuous flow of blood, you have a continuous problem of being ritually unclean, not to mention feeling weak. Besides that, there is the problem that some will think that this must have been caused by someone's sin, presumably my own. And of course this whole malady alienates me from the very people I would normally hope to be close to—family, friends, neighbors, synagogue attenders. It's hard to remain faithful, when you have to keep doing ritual purification rites every day, sometimes several times a day. You get a reputation of being unclean all the time, and people see you at the mikveh.

The word got around that the Galilean healer, Yeshua, was coming to town. You know how these rumors start, but in this case, it was true. Now we Galileans know something about prophetic healers. We have all heard the stories about Elijah and Elisha, as told by our parents, since early childhood. We had no trouble believing G-d might have raised up another such healer in our midst. But of course the real question was—Would he heal me in particular? After what seems like an eternity of putting up with this hemorrhaging, doubts creep into your mind and you start thinking that it could never get any better. You become frantic, and willing to try anything—anointing, immersion in a particularly clear body of water, prayer, touching of a holy cloth that belongs to a holy man. Most anything reasonable you become willing to try, even at the risk of public humiliation. I had decided that I did not care if I was rebuked for trying to touch Yeshua, I was going to make an effort, no matter what the obstacles.

I had not counted on the huge crowds. First of all there were his disciples, both male, and shockingly some females as well. I had never heard of a prophet or priest or teacher or scribe who had female followers. That must have caused tongues to wag. Some teachers even said it was morally wrong to teach women some of the finer points of Torah. I heard one say that women were too scatter-brained to take it in—the usual calumny against women, even pious women.

It was a hot mid-summer morning when Yeshua arrived, and the streets were lined with people, almost like it is during pilgrimage season when we go up to the festivals in Jerusalem. I am short compared to some men and women, and I was having trouble seeing, but throwing caution to the wind, and not worrying about what people might say that I brushed up against, I maneuvered myself into a spot where I could reach out and touch the tallith—in fact the very tassels on the hem of his prayer shawl. I must digress at this point, because, as you may know, years later, one of the disciples came and asked me about my story of healing. Here is what he wrote about it, and he tells the story better than I could . . .

"A large crowd followed and pressed around him. And a woman was there who had been subject to bleeding for twelve years. She had suffered a great deal under the care of many doctors and had spent all she had, yet instead of getting better she grew worse. When she heard about Yeshua, she came up behind him in the crowd and touched his cloak, because she thought, 'If I just touch his clothes, I will be healed.' Immediately her bleeding stopped and she felt in her body that she was freed from her suffering.

9

"At once Yeshua realized that power had gone out from him. He turned around in the crowd and asked, 'Who touched my clothes?'

"'You see the people crowding against you,' his disciples answered, 'and yet you can ask, "Who touched me?"'"

"But Yeshua kept looking around to see who had done it. Then the woman, knowing what had happened to her, came and fell at his feet and, trembling with fear, told him the whole truth. He said to her, 'Daughter, your faith has healed you. Go in peace and be freed from your suffering.'" [Mark 5]

Years later, when Mark came to ask me about this story, I tried to remember all I could, but it had been many years, and I am a very old woman now, not able to move about like I used to do. The thing that most stuck with me from that encounter was not only Yeshua calling me a daughter, even though I was older than he was, but his stressing that it was not some ritual or holy cloth that had healed me, but rather my reaching out in faith to touch him. I suppose before I had had a rather superstitious belief that the garments of the holy ones themselves could heal, but Yeshua wanted me to know it was through faith and a personal interaction with Him, that it happened. I never forgot that. Yeshua did not want me to have a magic tainted faith, but rather a personal one.

I can tell you though I was very afraid when he summoned me. I had hoped to touch him, and quietly melt back into the crowd without drawing any more attention to myself, than I had previously, due to my condition. I was tired of the scorn, and the superior attitudes, and the harsh judgments directed at me. Very tired of it. But Yeshua called me out of the crowd. He wanted me to know exactly how the healing had come.

Years later when someone read to me Mark's account, I realized something else. Many people pressed against Yeshua on that day, and nothing special happened to them. But they were not reaching out to Him in hopes of healing, not reaching out to Him in faith of any sort. They were just caught up in the moment and enjoying the celebration and the experience. Mark told me that Yeshua could actually feel, sense, the healing power, the energy going out of Him to someone, but he did not know who got the benefit. He had to ask. It was such a human moment for me, but I think also for Him. I was afraid, so afraid, I was going to be scolded again, told to get away from other people again.

But Yeshua was not like that. I reached out to Him, and something happened. It was not his touching me, but rather the reverse, and the power came forth from him almost involuntarily, but he sensed that it had happened and inquired about it. I must confess, I don't really understand this. Was it Yeshua himself, or was it power from G-d's Spirit flowing through Yeshua? In the end, it does not matter, since it was from G-d. And it totally changed my life.

I was too old for marriage, but I was able to present myself to the local priest and be officially declared clean. I could begin to have normal relations with people. And the oddest thing happened—I became something of a local celebrity—people came from all around wanting to hear about my healing. Many of them marveled that it could come after twelve years of suffering. Some of them went away in wonder saying "so G-d has indeed again visited his people through Yeshua." Some people even became his followers partly because of my testimony.

The light is dimming now for me, and I know the day is not far off when I will be gathered to my ancestors, like all those before me. I don't see as well as I used to, walk as well as I used to, eat as well as I used to. I remember the words of the Scriptures . . .

> Remember your Creator
> in the days of your youth,
> before the days of trouble come
> and the years approach when you will say,
> "I find no pleasure in them"—
> before the sun and the light
> and the moon and the stars grow dark,
> and the clouds return after the rain;
> when the keepers of the house tremble,
> and the strong men stoop,
> when the grinders cease because they are few,
> and those looking through the windows grow dim;
> when the doors to the street are closed
> and the sound of grinding fades;
> when people rise up at the sound of birds,
> but all their songs grow faint;
> when people are afraid of heights
> and of dangers in the streets;
> when the almond tree blossoms
> and the grasshopper drags itself along
> and desire no longer is stirred.

Then people go to their eternal home
and mourners go about the streets. [Ecclesiastes 12]

I memorized this passage in my youth, and it has stayed with me ever since. Now I understand the symbolism better than I used to do. The grinders are of course the teeth, the windows are the eyes, and I don't hear as well as I used to, but in my mind I can still hear that gentle yet powerful voice say "daughter your faith has healed you." I know all too well about sleepless nights when any noise can awaken me, and I cannot climb the step to the roof of my house for fear of falling. My hands tremble, and the desires of youth are no longer stirred. No matter, I am in G-d's hands, and have joy in my heart. I remember my Creator even now, and I am thankful for the day his Son passed my way. In a lifetime there are many important moments, many peaks and valleys, many joys and sorrows, but the day I was healed was a one of a kind day—and its blessing has stayed with me even until now.

CHAPTER THREE

THE PARALYTIC

IT'S A HORRIBLE THING TO LOSE YOUR MOBILITY. TO NOT BE ABLE TO EVEN get up and relieve yourself without having help. Horrible. You feel so totally helpless, and you feel like you are a huge burden to those around you, your loved ones, your friends, your neighbors. You have to keep asking for favors—"Would you please bring me some water? Could you just hand me that tool?" and on and on and on. It's humiliating for a man like me, indeed for anyone. You lose your self-respect, your sense of dignity, and you become just mad at the world, perhaps even mad at G-d. You're constantly moaning and groaning. And then, no one wants to be around you. They tiptoe around you, or in trying to be helpful they become patronizing . . . "Here, let me do that for you friend . . ." You know what I mean. You lie around or sit around all day and you develop bed sores, in places I'm not going to mention, so that even just sitting isn't comfortable anymore.

One day my family and neighbors decided to do something about this whole situation. There was now a healer living just down the road in Capernaum. They believed he could help me. I had no such confidence, but I could hardly object. On the remote chance something good might happen, I realized that the worst that could happen is I would be humiliated in public. But I was already used to that, ever since the day I fell off the roof of our house and then couldn't get up and walk again. Some man named Mark later wrote about what happened, and it captures the essence of that moment . . .

"*A few days later, when Yeshua again entered Capernaum, the people heard that he had come home. They gathered in such large numbers that there was no room left, not even outside the door, and he preached the word to them. Some men came, bringing to him a paralyzed man, carried by four of them. Since they could not get him to Yeshua because of the crowd, they made an opening in the roof above Yeshua by digging through it and then lowered the mat the man was lying on. When Yeshua saw their faith, he said to the paralyzed man, 'Son, your sins are forgiven.'*

"*Now some teachers of the law were sitting there, thinking to themselves, 'Why does this fellow talk like that? He's blaspheming! Who can forgive sins but G-d alone?'*

"*Immediately Yeshua knew in his spirit that this was what they were thinking in their hearts, and he said to them, 'Why are you thinking these things? Which is easier: to say to this paralyzed man, "Your sins are forgiven," or to say, "Get up, take your mat and walk"? But I want you to know that the Son of Man has authority on earth to forgive sins.' So he said to the man, 'I tell you, get up, take your mat and go home.' He got up, took his mat and walked out in full view of them all. This amazed everyone and they praised G-d, saying, 'We have never seen anything like this!'*" [Mark 2]

This healer Yeshua had set up shop, so to speak, in the house of Simon's mother-in-law in Capernaum. He made it his homebase from which he traveled around Galilee, teaching, preaching, and healing. He actually was from another Galilean town, a smaller one called Nazareth. Anyway, he now resided near me, and so many people were giving testimonies to what he could do, that, when my friends and family insisted on taking me to him . . . Well, I just went along for the ride, so to speak.

Now when we got there, the place was packed with people needing help. There were people with bad eyesight, people with skin diseases, people with broken limbs, bent backs, all kinds of people needing help. When I saw the crowd, I said to my four bearers, "Let's just go back home. He's too busy now. It can wait. I'm not in any danger of suddenly getting worse." But they were determined to get me in to see Yeshua. They climbed up on the roof of this house, which had a courtyard. Part of the courtyard had been shaded with brush so members of the family could sit outside and weave or do some other task like gutting fish, without the sun bearing down on them. My bearers peeled back the brush, and lowered me ever so carefully into the presence of Yeshua. People were shouting "Watch out!" and the like, but finally I was on the ground, in front of Yeshua.

I'll be honest, I expected Yeshua to lay hands on my legs or anoint them and pray, or just pray for my healing, but none of that happened! Instead, Yeshua said something completely unexpected. Out of the blue he said, "Son your sins have been forgiven." Now, this was shocking. As the teachers there remarked, only G-d can forgive sin, so they accused Yeshua of blasphemy! You could feel the tension there suddenly rise. It is interesting that Yeshua spoke in the passive. He could have meant by it—"G-d has forgiven your sins already," but then—How would he know this? I had not offered any sacrifices lately, nor had I repented of my sins. G-d and I were actually not on that good of terms at the moment. I was angry with Him.

Then Yeshua got into an argument, a debate with those teachers who objected to his pronouncement. Yeshua then asked them a question— "Which is easier—to say your sins are forgiven, or rise, take up your pallet and walk?" Well the teachers had no ready answer to that brain-teaser, and I kind of enjoyed watching them squirm and puzzle over his question. I reckon it's easier to say "Your sins are forgiven," because who can tell if it's true or not? There's no immediate physical evidence of the fact. But as to which is easier to do—well that's got to be healing limbs. Even ordinary human physicians can sometimes help with that. But no one but G-d can do the more difficult task of forgiving sins, or so I thought until then. But then, it was my turn to squirm, because Yeshua gave me an order, "Rise, take up your pallet and walk." At first I thought this was ridiculous because he wasn't even lending a helping hand, he wanted me to try it on my own. But then unexpectedly I felt my legs again. I felt some strength come back into my shriveled limbs. So I decided I would give it a try. When I stood, I wobbled a bit, but I was able to manage it, and I used the little pallet to brace myself on for a second and then, to everyone's astonishment, including mine, I walked right out of the building! I was mobile again. I could work again. I wasn't useless any more, all thanks to Yeshua and G-d.

After the fact, it became clear that Yeshua was responding to the faith and trust of my family and friends who brought me to him. I am still not sure what to make of his claim to be the "Son of Man" who has authority to forgive sins, but that he is a healer, there can be no doubt. No doubt at all. I am the living proof. I am Exhibit A that G-d must be with him. In a more reflective moment I also realized that I had been sinning against G-d and my family by all my complaining and anger. G-d had not done this to me, rather it was a result of my own carelessness. I realized then why Yeshua had said first—"Your sins are forgiven." It was because that was my greater need, to be at one with my Maker. People can say what they want about Yeshua, but this I know. He could not do the things he has done all over the land if G-d were not with him. That's just the truth.

CHAPTER FOUR

THE HARLOT

If there's one thing I despise, it's hypocrisy. Men come to me with their needs and wants, their desires to be pleasured in the dark of the night, but of course discreetly, as they don't want to be shamed. It's the married men who are the worst. They sneak around, they enjoy themselves, and then in public they condemn harlotry! Simon the Pharisee was one of those sorts of men. Oh yes, he knew me alright, knew what kind of person I was, *by personal experience.* While he never visited me, he knew his brother did and he said not a word. Nothing!

Yeshua, on the other hand, was a very different sort of man. He never came to me wanting something like that. He came to me because I was broken, ashamed, needing help and healing. And he even offered forgiveness. I was so very grateful. I broke into tears when he told me I could be forgiven. I wanted to do something, an act of gratitude, the next time he

17

passed through town. And I did. This is how a later storyteller told my tale
. . .

*"When one of the Pharisees invited Yeshua to have dinner with him, he
went to the Pharisee's house and reclined at the table. A woman in that town
who lived a sinful life learned that Yeshua was eating at the Pharisee's house,
so she came there with an alabaster jar of perfume. As she stood behind him
at his feet weeping, she began to wet his feet with her tears. Then she wiped
them with her hair, kissed them and poured perfume on them.*

*"When the Pharisee who had invited him saw this, he said to himself, "If
this man were a prophet, he would know who is touching him and what kind
of woman she is—that she is a sinner."*

"Yeshua answered him, 'Simon, I have something to tell you.'

'Tell me, teacher,' he said.

*'Two people owed money to a certain moneylender. One owed him five
hundred denarii, and the other fifty. Neither of them had the money to pay
him back, so he forgave the debts of both. Now which of them will love him
more?'*

Simon replied, 'I suppose the one who had the bigger debt forgiven.'

'You have judged correctly,' Yeshua said.

*"Then he turned toward the woman and said to Simon, 'Do you see this
woman? I came into your house. You did not give me any water for my feet,
but she wet my feet with her tears and wiped them with her hair. You did not
give me a kiss, but this woman, from the time I entered, has not stopped kissing my feet. You did not put oil on my head, but she has poured perfume on
my feet. Therefore, I tell you, her many sins have been forgiven—as her great
love has shown. But whoever has been forgiven little loves little.'*

"Then Yeshua said to her, 'Your sins are forgiven.'

*"The other guests began to say among themselves, 'Who is this who even
forgives sins?'*

"Yeshua said to the woman, 'Your faith has saved you; go in peace.'"
[Luke 7]

It was summer time. The heat was extreme, and when someone comes
off those hot dusty roads, the normal custom is to have a servant or a
member of the household not merely welcome a guest, but have their feet
washed, and their scalp anointed to prevent cracking and pain. Simon apparently had done neither of these things when Yeshua arrived at his house.
If you are wondering how I gained entrance, in the summer the houses are
wide open during the day to allow for ventilation. You can see in, you can

hear, you can walk right in because none of the doors are shut. And so I did. I walked right into the house. The dining area was in the big family living area that was in the front of the house, so as to get the breeze. Yeshua and Simon were deep in conversation, reclining on couches and at first Simon did not see me. I stooped down at the end of the couch where Yeshua was and began anointing his feet with my best perfume. I also began to cry. I had been so moved, so grateful, so relieved after my previous conversation with Yeshua. In fact, I had been so strongly motivated, I had become determined to give up my lucrative profession, and start afresh in life. I had enough resources to move to another town where my reputation would not have preceded me. But I waited until this day to make the move, because I was afraid I would miss Yeshua's coming, since he passed through this seaside village regularly.

I am still amazed at the way Yeshua handled the critique of Simon. He didn't rebut Simon's mutterings about Yeshua being spiritually obtuse and not knowing what kind of person I was. Instead, as was his habit, he told a story, a story about debt and forgiveness. And he is right. A person who has been forgiven more, is more grateful, is likely to show more love. Yeshua implied I had indeed been forgiven more, and therefore was responding to the grace with more gratitude than Simon had. But I did notice that Yeshua was implying Simon had a need for forgiveness as well. Oh yes, he was a community leader, and yet he was prepared to be silent and overlook the sins of his brother with me while condemning me. That's just sheer hypocrisy and Yeshua didn't like it any better than I did.

"G-d is no respecter of persons," he once said. G-d couldn't care less about a person's honor or status in a community. He does not dole out justice or mercy on the basis of such all too human considerations. I freely granted I needed a lot of forgiveness, but then, so does everyone. We all sin and fall short. Instead of pointing a finger at me, Yeshua held out a hand and said, "Daughter, you can do better, receive the forgiveness of sins and go and sin no more." And on this occasion he added—"Your faith has set you free. Go with the shalom of G-d—the wholeness, the well-being, the peace of G-d." I am determined to do so, starting today.

CHAPTER FIVE

THE MAN BORN BLIND

IT IS IMPOSSIBLE TO TELL YOU WHAT TOTAL DARKNESS IS LIKE UNLESS YOU have spent a long time deep in one of those caves in the cliffs of Arbel near the sea of Galilee. Your mind still has ideas about shapes of things since you can pick them up and feel them, but even the sense of touch can be deceptive. You remember the old story about three blind men who approached an elephant and were asked what he was like. One touched the elephant's ear and said an elephant is like a large palm leaf. Another felt the elephant's tusk and said the elephant was like a shophar, a ram's horn which we hollow out and use as a horn to blow at festival time. Still another one felt the elephant's tail and said an elephant was like a rope. Of course they were all basically wrong. The elephant as a whole was not really very much like any of these things.

But there are other problems with being blind besides not being able to figure out the outside world. If you are a devout person and you keep hearing the stories in Torah about G-d's light which he created, G-d's revelation which is sometimes called light, you feel left out because you have never seen the light, nor can you read about it. You can only listen to others tell about it. It makes you feel like you have been left out of G-d's plans. The Scriptures may say, "The people who dwell in darkness have seen a great light," but I could never say that before Yeshua came along and put mud on my eyes. And even then few would know my story if Yeshua had not come to me again after I was expelled from the synagogue so I could see him finally face to face, and honor him for what he had done. Even then, few would know my tale if it had not been for Yeshua's Beloved Disciple, Eleazar, who lived near me, in Bethany, and asked me, some years after Yeshua had gone to be with G-d, about what had happened. Here is how he told my story . . .

"As Yeshua went along, he saw a man blind from birth. His disciples asked him, 'Rabbi, who sinned, this man or his parents, that he was born blind?'

"'Neither this man nor his parents sinned,' said Yeshua, 'but this happened so that the works of G-d might be displayed in him. As long as it is day, we must do the works of him who sent me. Night is coming, when no one can work. While I am in the world, I am the light of the world.'

"After saying this, he spit on the ground, made some mud with the saliva, and put it on the man's eyes. 'Go,' he told him, 'wash in the Pool of Siloam' (this word means "Sent"). So the man went and washed, and came home seeing.

"His neighbors and those who had formerly seen him begging asked, 'Isn't this the same man who used to sit and beg?' Some claimed that he was.

"Others said, 'No, he only looks like him.'

"But he himself insisted, 'I am the man.'

"'How then were your eyes opened?' they asked.

"He replied, 'The man they call Yeshua made some mud and put it on my eyes. He told me to go to Siloam and wash. So I went and washed, and then I could see.'

"'Where is this man?' they asked him.

"'I don't know,' he said.

"They brought to the Pharisees the man who had been blind. Now the day on which Yeshua had made the mud and opened the man's eyes was a

Sabbath. Therefore the Pharisees also asked him how he had received his sight. 'He put mud on my eyes,' the man replied, 'and I washed, and now I see.'

"Some of the Pharisees said, 'This man is not from G-d, for he does not keep the Sabbath.'

"But others asked, 'How can a sinner perform such signs?' So they were divided.

"Then they turned again to the blind man, 'What have you to say about him? It was your eyes he opened.'

"The man replied, 'He is a prophet.'

"They still did not believe that he had been blind and had received his sight until they sent for the man's parents. 'Is this your son?' they asked. 'Is this the one you say was born blind? How is it that now he can see?'

"'We know he is our son,' the parents answered, 'and we know he was born blind. But how he can see now, or who opened his eyes, we don't know. Ask him. He is of age; he will speak for himself.' His parents said this because they were afraid of the Jewish leaders, who already had decided that anyone who acknowledged that Yeshua was the Messiah would be put out of the synagogue. That was why his parents said, 'He is of age; ask him.'

"A second time they summoned the man who had been blind. 'Give glory to G-d by telling the truth,' they said. 'We know this man is a sinner.'

"He replied, 'Whether he is a sinner or not, I don't know. One thing I do know. I was blind but now I see!'

"Then they asked him, 'What did he do to you? How did he open your eyes?'

"He answered, 'I have told you already and you did not listen. Why do you want to hear it again? Do you want to become his disciples too?'

"Then they hurled insults at him and said, 'You are this fellow's disciple! We are disciples of Moses! We know that G-d spoke to Moses, but as for this fellow, we don't even know where he comes from.'

"The man answered, 'Now that is remarkable! You don't know where he comes from, yet he opened my eyes. We know that G-d does not listen to sinners. He listens to the godly person who does his will. Nobody has ever heard of opening the eyes of a man born blind. If this man were not from G-d, he could do nothing.'

"To this they replied, 'You were steeped in sin at birth; how dare you lecture us!' And they threw him out.

"Yeshua heard that they had thrown him out, and when he found him, he said, 'Do you believe in the Son of Man?'

"'Who is he, sir?' the man asked. 'Tell me so that I may believe in him.'

"Yeshua said, 'You have now seen him; in fact, he is the one speaking with you.'

"Then the man said, 'Lord, I believe,' and he worshiped him.

"Yeshua said, 'For judgment I have come into this world, so that the blind will see and those who see will become blind.'

"Some Pharisees who were with him heard him say this and asked, 'What? Are we blind too?'

"Yeshua said, 'If you were blind, you would not be guilty of sin; but now that you claim you can see, your guilt remains.'" [John 9]

It was true, that there are no miracles in the Torah about sight being given to a person born blind. It was also true that some of our teachers had said that a person who could do that must be G-d's anointed, or at least the last great Elijah-like prophet who was to come before the Day of the Lord. So I was very ready to recognize Yeshua by whatever title he preferred.

Yet it is ironic that my newfound sight, as great a blessing as it was, created immediate problems for me—I was not prepared to denounce my Healer, and I was also not prepared for my parents to not stand up for me. I became a man expelled from the two places I most wanted to be—my home and my synagogue.

Fortunately, some of Yeshua's followers came to me not long after his death and resurrection and persuaded me to join their number. I was happy to have a spiritual family again. I learned the meaning of the saying of Yeshua—"Do not think that I came to bring peace on the earth; I did not come to bring peace, but a sword. For I came to set a man against his father, and a daughter against her mother, and a daughter-in-law against her mother-in-law; and a man's enemies will be the members of his own household" [Matthew 10]. Such was the price I paid for becoming a follower of Yeshua. It was a heavy price to pay.

As Yeshua suggested, there is more than one kind of blindness, and the worst kind is spiritual blindness, not physical blindness. Even worse still is claiming to have seen the light of G-d, and in fact not telling the truth about it. This is why Yeshua said what he did about those Pharisees, who elsewhere he called play-actors, hypocrites who appear to be and act one way, but actually are another. Their spiritual blindness was not allowed as an excuse since they claimed to "see" truly the things of G-d. There is nothing worse than the spiritual blind becoming leaders, leading those who are blind, not yet enlightened. This is an even greater darkness than I have ever experienced.

Sometime later, the Beloved Disciple shared a saying he had written about Yeshua, and it speaks of both the tragedy and the triumph that came from his appearing—

"The true light that gives light to everyone was coming into the world. He was in the world, and though the world was made through him, the world did not recognize him. He came to that which was his own, but his own did not receive him. Yet to all who did receive him, to those who believed in his name, he gave the right to become children of G-d—children born not of natural descent, nor of human decision or a husband's will, but born of G-d." [John 1]

Though I am old now, I feel like my life began over again, when I first splashed water from the Pool of Siloam on my face, and began to see, truly see, the meaning of my life. I have often wondered why Yeshua gave me the task of going to the pool and washing out my eyes, when he could have just touched me. But lately it has dawned on me that perhaps he wanted me to participate in my own healing. If you don't you will never be enlightened, never understand. Thank G-d I both began to see the light, and began to understand who the true light of the world was, on that day.

CHAPTER SIX

JAIRUS'S DAUGHTER

SOME HAVE SAID LOSING A DAUGHTER IS NOT THE SAME AS LOSING A SON. They say that daughters are less important than sons in terms of inheritance, property, building the family name and legacy. They even say daughters are less useful than sons when it comes to farming, or practicing a trade. Some have even said daughters should not be educated, not be taught the Torah. They are simply to be prepared to be betrothed to some worthy Torah true young man who is the member of a good family. That will bring more honor to one's own family, and hopefully more resources as well. To those from whom I hear such dictums I say—"Shame on you! Daughters are as much a gift from G-d as sons, and in some ways can be even more valuable than a son." Have such people never read the story of Ruth or even Esther or Judith?[1]

---

1. The book of Judith is an extra-canonical early Jewish book that is found in the

It is one thing to lose a child in childbirth. This happens a lot in our world, and it is always a sadness, a tragedy. But to lose a daughter whom you have had years with, have watched grow up, have prayed with, fed, clothed, raised for twelve years—that is a different matter! You can understand then why I was frantic to find the Healer named Yeshua when our twelve-year-old daughter Dodai fell deathly ill. Later, I had a scribe, who worked in my village and synagogue, write down the story of that remarkable day, because he wrote much more eloquently than I could. Here is how he presented things.

"*When Yeshua had again crossed over by boat to the other side of the lake, a large crowd gathered around him while he was by the lake. Then one of the synagogue leaders, named Jairus, came, and when he saw Yeshua, he fell at his feet.*

He pleaded earnestly with him, 'My little daughter is dying. Please come and put your hands on her so that she will be healed and live.' So Yeshua went with him."

I must interrupt the telling of the story at this juncture to explain that something remarkable happened that delayed Yeshua in making it to my house. There was an absolutely huge crowd pressing around us. The need for healing by so many was so great, because the physicians are not very good, that Yeshua was thronged by crowds wherever he went. This was one such occasion. As it turns out, there was a woman with an issue of blood, who touched Yeshua, needing healing, and she was almost instantly healed. But Yeshua, being a good teacher of our faith, stopped to make sure that the woman understood what or whom had healed her. He did not want her to have some kind of magic-tainted faith—as if the mere garments of a holy man could heal someone!

You can imagine, however, how deeply conflicted I felt when this woman caused a delay in Yeshua arriving at my house. The sense of panic was growing and growing within me, but I dared not interrupt an act of healing when that is what I longed for, for my daughter as well. It seemed to take an excruciatingly long time before Yeshua was ready to move again towards my house. Finally, when this happened horrible news arrived! This is how my chronicler put it . . .

Greek OT (the LXX), and is included in Catholic and Orthodox canons as a deuteron-canonical text. It tells the story of a Jewish heroine who lures and then beheads a pagan general named Holofernes. It seems to be based in part on the much older tale of Deborah and Jael found in Judges 4.

"Some people came from the house of Jairus, the synagogue leader. 'Your daughter is dead,' they said. 'Why bother the teacher anymore?'

"Overhearing what they said, Yeshua told him, 'Don't be afraid; just believe.'

"Yeshua did not let anyone follow him except Peter, Jacob, and John the brother of Jacob. When they came to the home of the synagogue leader, Yeshua saw a commotion, with people crying and wailing loudly. He went in and said to them, 'Why all this commotion and wailing? The child is not dead but asleep.' But they laughed at him.

"After he put them all out, he took the child's father and mother and the disciples who were with him, and went in where the child was. He took her by the hand and said to her, 'Talitha koum' (which means 'Little girl, I say to you, get up!'). Immediately the girl stood up and began to walk around (she was twelve years old). At this they were completely astonished. He gave strict orders not to let anyone know about this, and told them to give her something to eat." [Mark 5]

As you might imagine, at the end of this sequence of events, my wife and I had gone from being crushed to being overjoyed. But there are some things about the story the chronicler did not explain, which I want to make clear now.

Firstly, you need to understand our mourning customs. More well-to-do families hire professional mourners when someone dies, and this usually involves some women who weep and wail at the house, and later at the grave, and there is a flute player who plays mournful music. This goes on for about a week. Sometimes friends and relatives will come and sit Shiva with the family, which means that they simply come, bring food, and sit silently with the family and mourn with them.

In our case, however, the mourners showed up before we even had time to consider asking them to come. Ours is a small village, and word spreads quickly, and those folks saw an opportunity to make a little money, and so they showed up unannounced. I bring this up because as the scribe told the story, he mentioned that some people laughed when Yeshua said "She is not dead, she is sleeping." It was not members of my family, it was the professional mourners! You could tell they were not really invested in mourning with us, they were just hoping to get paid.

Another thing that I would like to make clear is what Yeshua meant when he spoke about death and sleeping. Our daughter was really dead, but Yeshua was someone who believed in resurrection, indeed he not merely

believed in it—he made it happen! The point is, those who believe in resurrection see death as no more permanent than sleep, and so they call it
"sleep"—something you come back from renewed and refreshed, good as
new. Yeshua was not suggesting that when you die you fall asleep. Indeed
his famous parable about the rich man and Lazarus makes clear he doesn't
believe we will be sleeping in the afterlife.

One of the things that most impressed me about Yeshua is that he had
no interest in dramatically performing the healing of Dodai in front of a big
crowd. He did not seem to want to draw attention to himself by performing
miracles. Rather he did them purely as acts of compassion. So it was that
he brought only three of his disciples into our house to witness the miracle,
along with my wife and myself. But there were more things that impressed
me about him.

Yeshua addressed Dodai as a person. He said in Aramaic, "talitha
cumi," which means "little girl arise." He knew she was a person, and should
not be treated like a mere object or a corpse. I can tell you we shouted when
she sat up, and there were tears of joy. But then he said, "Give her something to eat." He was concerned about her ongoing well-being. He wasn't
concerned with getting any credit or honor for this act, he was concerned
that she get the healing. I came to the conclusion later that Yeshua performed this great miracle the way he did to protect Dodai from becoming a
sort of spectacle and someone to gossip about. No one would know exactly
what happened to her other than the five of us, and of course we would
explain it to our beloved daughter, and only to those we could trust. Just as
Yeshua had said about the woman with the flow of blood, so it was also true
that our daughter was of sacred worth, a daughter of Abraham, precious
in the sight of G-d. I don't care what others may say about Yeshua, what I
know is that G-d was with him. No one could raise the dead if G-d were
not with him.

CHAPTER SEVEN

NICODEMUS

I STILL HAVEN'T TAKEN IT ALL IN. YOU KNOW HOW IT IS WHEN THINGS happen fast, and only later do you really grasp the significance of certain events, with the benefit of hindsight and considerable reflection. You have to understand I am a teacher, and so I do a lot of pondering anyway but Yeshua presented the biggest challenge ever to my understanding. I thought I had grasped even some of the deeper things of the Scriptures, and the more profound things of the faith, only to discover I needed to go back to square one and think through everything again.

Yeshua's ministry lasted only about three years, and so the time between when I went and visited with him early on, and the time of his trial, execution, and burial was not all that long. One moment I was marveling at his insight, the next moment I was dragging a huge bag of spices to put in the winding sheet for his burial. To say the least this juxtaposition was unsettling and disturbing.

And then there was the aftermath—all these former disciples of Yeshua, and even others like Jacob,[1] his brother, claiming they had seen Yeshua alive after his burial! I believe in resurrection as much as the next Pharisee, but I did not expect it to happen until the end times when all the righteous would be raised together as a group as Yeshua once suggested [John 5:28–29]. I have known Jacob now for many years in Jerusalem after the death of his brother, and he is still Torah true, and still insisting his brother is indeed the messiah! Something clearly changed him after the crucifixion, because before then he thought Yeshua was perhaps just another miracle worker [John 7:5]. Jacob had not been a disciple of Yeshua during his ministry. And something even more unsettling came much later, when my fellow Pharisee, Saul of Tarsus *also claimed* to have seen a risen and ascended Yeshua! I could hardly make sense of this at all, because Saul had been such an adamant opponent of "the Way" as it was called, and he persecuted the followers of Yeshua, not listening to the advice of my fellow teacher in Jerusalem, Gamaliel [see Acts 5:33–42]. And now, now apparently there are many many gentiles who have joined the Yeshua movement all across the empire. I ask myself—Is it possible that Yeshua was really the Jewish messiah, and indeed the light unto the nations, and are his followers carrying out G-d's will?

But the latest marvel, is that I have been handed a document written by one of the eyewitnesses of Yeshua's ministry, a man I once knew because he formerly lived in Bethany in the shadow of Jerusalem. He was named Eliezer[2] and was called the Beloved Disciple by Yeshua. I am an old man now, very old indeed, and it would appear I have become well-known to many followers of Yeshua, having become part of his story! This, I could never have imagined. For what it's worth, here is what the narrative says . . .

"Now there was a Pharisee, a man named Nicodemus who was a member of the Jewish ruling council. He came to Yeshua at night and said, 'Rabbi, we know that you are a teacher who has come from G-d. For no one could perform the signs you are doing if G-d were not with him.'

---

1. The man we know as James, the brother of the Lord, was in fact actually named Jacob. All of the James in the NT are actually Jacobs. The English name James comes as a result of the translation of Jacob into Spanish as Jaime, and thence to English as James.

2. This is the Hebrew form of the name Lazarus.

"Yeshua replied, 'Very truly I tell you, no one can see the kingdom of G-d unless they are born again.'

"'How can someone be born when they are old?' Nicodemus asked. 'Surely they cannot enter a second time into their mother's womb to be born!'

"Yeshua answered, 'Very truly I tell you, no one can enter the kingdom of G-d unless they are born of water and the Spirit. Flesh gives birth to flesh, but the Spirit gives birth to spirit. You should not be surprised at my saying, "You must be born again." The wind blows wherever it pleases. You hear its sound, but you cannot tell where it comes from or where it is going. So it is with everyone born of the Spirit.

"'How can this be?' Nicodemus asked.

"'You are Israel's teacher,' said Yeshua, 'and do you not understand these things? Very truly I tell you, we speak of what we know, and we testify to what we have seen, but still you people do not accept our testimony. I have spoken to you of earthly things and you do not believe; how then will you believe if I speak of heavenly things? No one has ever gone into heaven except the one who came from heaven—the Son of Man. Just as Moses lifted up the snake in the wilderness, so the Son of Man must be lifted up, that everyone who believes may have eternal life in him.'

"'For G-d loved the world in this fashion—he gave his one and only Son, that whoever believes in him shall not perish but have eternal life. For G-d did not send his Son into the world to condemn the world, but to save the world through him. Whoever believes in him is not condemned, but whoever does not believe stands condemned already because they have not believed in the name of G-d's one and only Son. This is the verdict: Light has come into the world, but people loved darkness instead of light because their deeds were evil. Everyone who does evil hates the light, and will not come into the light for fear that their deeds will be exposed. But whoever lives by the truth comes into the light, so that it may be seen plainly that what they have done has been done in the sight of G-d." [John 3]

There are a lot things I could say about this exchange, which certainly doesn't portray me in a very flattering light, but it is, I'm sad to say, an accurate portrait. I really was astonished and bewildered by Yeshua's suggestion that even pious old Jews needed to start over, be born again of G-d's Spirit. It took me a good while to puzzle out some of what he said, and I am happy to have this account to refresh my memory. You see most people in my world don't believe that people can radically change in their adult lives. We have sayings like "Can a leopard change its spots?" and the answer to the questions is decidedly in the negative. And yet if Saul could radically change then it must be possible for anyone, with G-d's help.

Yeshua must have related the incident to Eliezar sometime later. I did figure out that when Yeshua was talking about birth "out of water" he was referring to physical birth, not John's baptisms, and so the reference to birth again referred to a spiritual birth subsequent to physical birth. I had been wrong initially in assuming Yeshua was talking about two births of the same physical sort. He was not. I suppose it was because Yeshua, like John, saw Israel as so lost, having gone well astray, that there was a need to start all over with G-d.

A second odd thing about Yeshua's teaching is that he regularly prefaced one or another of his sayings with the word "Amen" and at the same time, he never cited one of his fellow or former Jewish teachers to support his claims. If one takes these two things together, they are quite astonishing because they suggest Yeshua thought his own words had inherent authority and didn't need the support of previous sages. Furthermore, the "Amening" of his own teaching suggested he could bear witness to the truthfulness of his own teaching, without needing a second party to pronounce the "so be it," the "Amen." Odd. And yet powerful. I shall not here delve into the mysteries of his comparison of his coming death with the lifting up of the snake image by Moses. These are some of the deeper things he said, which I have long pondered and still do not fully grasp.

Those last several sentences in the account which begins 'For G-d loved the world in this fashion' must be part of Eliezar's own later midrash on the significance of what Yeshua said and did during his ministry, for I do not remember Yeshua saying this on that occasion. He did not speak of himself in the third person like those sentences do, in my hearing. But this brings me to the other episode, a much sadder one that involved me in the story of Yeshua.

I was indeed a member of the Sanhedrin in Jerusalem. I was not present in Caiphas's house when the initial inquiry of Yeshua happened, but I was there later when the decision was taken after hearing witnesses. What really prompted the final judgment of Caiphas, was not the claim that Yeshua might be the messiah. It was not blasphemy to claim this possibility. No, it was what Yeshua said after that that caused the high priest to tear his robes and hand Yeshua over to Pontius Pilate. I shall never forget those words—"I am, and you will see the Son of Man seated at the right hand of power and coming on the clouds" [Mark 14:62]. We all knew that Yeshua regularly called himself "the Son of Man" and here he seemed to be claiming to have divine power and authority, and to be the one who would one day come on the "great and terrible day of the Lord" and judge the world. In other words, while Caiaphas thought he was judging Yeshua, Yeshua was threatening or promising to return as a divine figure and judge Caiaphas and others who had condemned him. This was too much for Caiaphas, and it was this that he claimed was blasphemy. Only G-d in person would one day come to judge the world. So it was that Yeshua was condemned and handed over to the Roman authorities. The chronicle picks up the story as follows . . .

"Now it was the day of Preparation, and the next day was to be a special Sabbath. Because the Jewish leaders did not want the bodies left on the crosses during the Sabbath, they asked Pilate to have the legs broken and the bodies taken down. The soldiers therefore came and broke the legs of the first man who had been crucified with Yeshua, and then those of the other. But when they came to Yeshua and found that he was already dead, they did not break his legs. Instead, one of the soldiers pierced Yeshua's side with a spear, bringing a sudden flow of blood and water. The man who saw it has given testimony, and his testimony is true. He knows that he tells the truth, and he testifies so that you also may believe. These things happened so that the scripture would be fulfilled: 'Not one of his bones will be broken,' and, as another scripture says, 'They will look on the one they have pierced.'

"Later, Joseph of Arimathea asked Pilate for the body of Yeshua. Now Joseph was a disciple of Yeshua, but secretly because he feared the Jewish leaders. With Pilate's permission, he came and took the body away. He was accompanied by Nicodemus, the man who earlier had visited Yeshua at night. Nicodemus brought a mixture of myrrh and aloes, about seventy-five pounds. Taking Yeshua's body, the two of them wrapped it, with the spices, in strips of linen. This was in accordance with Jewish burial customs. At the place where Yeshua was crucified, there was a garden, and in the garden a new tomb, in which no one had ever been laid. Because it was the Jewish day of Preparation and since the tomb was nearby, they laid Yeshua there." [John 19]

I was like a man in a daze, being totally in shock as to what happened to Yeshua. I am happy to have this fuller report from Eliezar, who stood bravely at the foot of the cross with Yeshua's mother when the Twelve had all abandoned, or denied, or betrayed Yeshua. Joseph of Arimathea was a good friend. Like him I had had such hopes for Yeshua, and, like him, I was longing for the inbreaking of G-d's saving reign, his kingdom. I had thought Yeshua might be the means of that, and like Joseph I had been silent when the vote went against Yeshua in the Sanhedrin. It was not just that we Jews did not want the body of our fellow Jew hanging on a cross during Passover, it was also that Joseph and I wanted to honor the good things Yeshua had said and done, even though our hearts were heavy, feeling like the crucifixion had to mean G-d had abandoned Yeshua, or even worse, had cursed him. Yet still we thought he deserved an honorable burial, and not have the outcome that a crucified Jew so often faced—being thrown in a ditch, or into a common unmarked grave. All the people that Yeshua had healed or helped or taught would not have wanted that.

Thus it was that Joseph approached Pilate, who was all too happy to get this sordid affair over with, and readily granted Joseph the disposing of the body. I went with Joseph to his own tomb, dragging a huge bag of spices. Honestly, without thinking I bought the quantity of spices that the spice merchant suggested, but later realized he was just trying to make a good sale, and he succeeded. I was in so much shock I didn't even haggle with him, I just paid. Later, it occurred to me that the only persons who were buried with this much spices in the burial shroud were kings, because their graves would be visited my lots of people during the week of mourning, and the spices were meant to retard the odor of the decaying corpse.

You might want to know what I thought about Joseph's tomb being empty only a day and half later. Well, for a start, we are all familiar with grave robbing. It is sadly an all too common practice, even in Judea. People desperate for resources ransack tombs hoping to find jewels and the like to sell in order to survive or thrive. But it is very, very unlikely this happened to Yeshua's tomb. We made very sure it was sealed with a huge rolling stone that no single or even two or three persons could readily move.

Something else must have happened to the body of Yeshua. And I can tell you many years later, that while many Jews who had been hostile to Yeshua looked and looked and tried to find his corpse, because they were afraid without that the Yeshua matter would not be "laid to rest," so to speak, no one ever found it. I say this decades later. Had the disciples reburied Yeshua somewhere else nearby, someone would have heard about it, someone would have found it, because Caiaphas had people searching for the body. Nothing was ever found, and now no one is looking. The case is closed.

Except of course it isn't, because the followers of Yeshua are growing in number, not dwindling. The proclamation about Yeshua has not been silenced, indeed one can hear of him now in many places in the Roman Empire. Recently, I was talking with a Jew from Roma and he told me there were many followers of Yeshua even there, at the heart of the empire. No other Jewish teacher, not even John the Baptizer, has so many followers these days. And the proclamation of his resurrection, and of his being alive in heaven, goes on and on and on. As for me, I am still praying and pondering about these things. I ask myself—Could these things really be true? Was, is, Yeshua the hope of Israel and light to the nations? Perhaps it is so. Perhaps I should have listened to the words of Gamaliel who said of the followers of Yeshua, "if their purpose or activity is of human origin, it will (eventually) fail. But if it is from G-d, you will not be able to stop these men, and you will find yourself fighting against G-d." [Acts 5:38–39] I have no desire to do that, none whatsoever. So . . . I will think more of what Yeshua first said to me—"Nicodemus, you must be born again."

CHAPTER EIGHT

MIRIAM AND MARTHA

I HAVE A COMPLAINT. WHY IS IT, IN ALL THE TELLINGS OF THE GOOD NEWS
the focus is almost always on the Galilean disciples of Yeshua? Do the
chroniclers really not remember that Yeshua also came regularly to Judea
and had Judean disciples as well? No, I'm not talking about the infamous
Judas from Kerioth, the one who betrayed Yeshua. I mean people like my
family—Miriam, Eliezar, and myself, Martha. Thank goodness Luke, the
sometime companion of Paul, and Eliezar have begun to redress the problem in their narratives. One might have thought Mark, the sometime companion of Peter and one time resident of Jerusalem would have addressed
this problem, or at least Matthew, who wrote for Jewish Christians. But no!
They did not really deal with this issue for whatever reason. Now that we
are a full generation and more since the death of Yeshua, it is high time that

our stories were told. True, we only get brief mention in Luke's account, but I'll take something over nothing. Here's what Luke said:

"As Yeshua and his disciples were on their way, he came to a village where a woman named Martha opened her home to him. She had a sister called Miriam, who sat at the Lord's feet listening to what he said. But Martha was distracted by all the preparations that had to be made. She came to him and asked, 'Lord, don't you care that my sister has left me to do the work by myself? Tell her to help me!'

"'Martha, Martha,' the Lord answered, 'you are worried and upset about many things, but only one thing is necessary. Miriam has chosen the good portion, and it will not be taken away from her.' [Luke 10]

I admit this story does not display me in the best possible light. But you may have forgotten just how important hospitality was in our world, and how it was not every day one got to have a famous Jewish healer and teacher in one's house. Furthermore, I had been trained to be a good hostess, and it seemed quite unfair for Miriam to simply sit in the larger room soaking up Yeshua's wisdom while I was slaving away, cooking things for our meal.

Yes, I know Yeshua has always had female disciples, and this is a good thing, a new thing in Judaism. He even has had traveling female disciples, which certainly set tongues wagging about Yeshua, since these were women he was not related to, and in some cases women who Yeshua had exorcised or healed. Miriam and I however were not among the traveling disciples. We were the stay-at-home disciples, and for a good reason. You will notice that Luke does not mention our brother Eliezar (also called Lazarus). I suspect this is because he was a physician and he didn't want to unnecessarily complicate the story, because it would require too much additional explaining. You see our father was Simon the leper, and not only did he die, our brother died as well of this dread disease. If you are wondering why three adult siblings are living together and none of them are married it is because of the fear of this horrible disease. I will let Miriam tell you more about that in a moment.

What you may not have noticed about this story is that while Yeshua was coming to Bethany with male and female disciples, only Yeshua entered our house and was prepared to eat with us. The rest decided not to enter. Luke apparently wanted to just focus on the famous final saying of Yeshua. Speaking of which, the saying is contrasting the many dishes I was preparing, and the one good portion Miriam had chosen. It was a clever saying, which has been misunderstood over the years. The one thing necessary is to be Yeshua's disciple and soak up his teachings. Everything else is secondary to that. But I've talked enough; here's my sister and her story.

***

I am indeed the more quiet and introspective one, the less outgoing sister. Martha tends to share her feelings openly, I am more reticent to do that. But there was one occasion where I threw caution to the wind, in order to honor Yeshua in our home. It was just after Yeshua had raised Eliezar from the dead. Interestingly, there is both a version of this story told by Mark, and another told by my brother. I will present you with both, but I can tell you, the latter account is more circumstantial and reveals more.

"While he was in Bethany, reclining at the table in the home of Simon the Leper, a woman came with an alabaster jar of very expensive perfume, made of pure nard. She broke the jar and poured the perfume on his head.

"Some of those present were saying indignantly to one another, 'Why this waste of perfume? It could have been sold for more than a year's wage and the money given to the poor.' And they rebuked her harshly.

"'Leave her alone,' said Yeshua. 'Why are you bothering her? She has done a beautiful thing to me. The poor you will always have with you, and you can help them any time you want. But you will not always have me. She did what she could. She poured perfume on my body beforehand to prepare for my burial. Truly I tell you, wherever the good news is preached throughout the world, what she has done will also be told, in memory of her.'" [Mark 14]

"Six days before the Passover, Yeshua came to Bethany, where Eliezar lived, whom Yeshua had raised from the dead. Here a dinner was given in Yeshua's honor. Martha served, while Eliezar was among those reclining at the table with him. Then Miriam took about half a litre of pure nard, an expensive perfume; she poured it on Yeshua's feet and wiped his feet with her hair. And the house was filled with the fragrance of the perfume.

"But one of his disciples, Judas Iscariot, who was later to betray him, objected, 'Why wasn't this perfume sold and the money given to the poor? It was worth a year's wages.' He did not say this because he cared about the poor but because he was a thief; as keeper of the money bag, he used to help himself to what was put into it.

"'Leave her alone,' Yeshua replied. 'It was intended that she should save this perfume for the day of my burial. You will always have the poor among you, but you will not always have me.'" [John 12]

Notice that Mark does not mention me by name, and he mentions Martha not at all, even though she was the hostess for the meal, as she had been before in the meal my sister spoke of earlier. While it was not unusual in our world for women to be left nameless in accounts all written by men, it is especially peculiar that Mark does so since he includes the saying of Yeshua about this story being told in memory of me wherever the gospel is preached! Extraordinary! Yet he does manage to mention that our father was leper. I wonder why he did that, but I'm sure it wasn't in order to shame our family. Perhaps it was because he wanted to show that Yeshua did not avoid people with dreaded diseases. He was a great healer.

I am a cautious person generally, but after Yeshua raised Eliezar, my heart was so filled with joy and gratitude I decided to do something extravagant as a way of saying thank you. You see if the man of the household dies, this becomes very problematic if only women remain behind, because women cannot inherit the property. It would pass to the next nearest male relative, and we might well find ourselves looking for a home. But Yeshua did not let that happen. He raised my brother from the dead who had been dead already four days—a very great miracle indeed, which called for a lavish response.

It is interesting that Mark does not tell us that Judas was the one who led the charge in protesting my extravagant gesture, but my brother's account makes this very clear. And Yeshua silenced him quickly enough, to be sure. Now pistic nard is the most expensive perfume around. Women use it for a variety of purposes, but honestly I had no thought of performing a burial ritual in advance. That was just how Yeshua came to interpret the significance of the act, and later I understood why he did so. There was no time on the day he died for us to properly honor him. By the time Eliezar got home, breathless with the horrible news of Yeshua's execution, it was too late for me to act. The Sabbath, and for that matter, the Passover was at hand. Such honoring and rituals had to wait.

Anointing oil may be regularly used on both the scalp and the feet, to prevent cracking due to the intense sun. Perfume can be used anywhere to overcome odor, or just as a way of honoring an important person. I wanted to use something more than just olive oil to anoint Yeshua. As for his famous response 'the poor you always have with you' this was not meant to provide his followers with an excuse for not helping the poor, especially not now that he is in heaven! It was meant to make clear that honoring him during his earthly ministry was more important at that time. It is a saying that has been misused since then by those looking for excuses not to help the poor, which would have appalled Yeshua. He said they were blessed by G-d. I am so glad I took the chance and opportunity to honor Yeshua and thank him in this way despite the extravagance and it being out of character for me, because as he said, "You will not always have me with you," and indeed it became true within days. But fortunately, that was not the end of his story.

CHAPTER NINE

THE GERASENE DEMONIAC

I AM NOT A JEW. NOR DID I BECOME A JEW AFTER YESHUA RESCUED ME from the malevolent spirits. I am simply a man who lives in a village on the non-Jewish side of the Sea of Tiberias. My story is not a pleasant one, and indeed it pains me to tell it, but I have told it many times in the Decapolis, the ten Greek cities which border the land of the Jews, to honor the request Yeshua made of me. Yeshua would not allow me to become one of his traveling companions and close disciples even though I literally begged him to let me go with him. Instead, he wanted me to tell my tale to those like me who were not Jews and not looking for a Jewish messiah. My story then is a story about Yeshua the mighty exorcist, who liberated me from the strong grasp of the powers of darkness. As I hinted, this is not a pleasant tale, rather it is a shocking one. Who is it who has power over the dark lords? Who is it that can set the person in spiritual bondage free? Who is it who even cares for an unclean soul who must live in graveyard full of unclean corpses and is so full of self-loathing that he constantly hurts himself even when he is chained to a spot? That was me. That was my story. Here is how a later follower of Yeshua told it.

"They went across the lake to the region of the Gerasenes. When Yeshua got out of the boat, a man with an impure spirit came from the tombs to meet him. This man lived in the tombs, and no one could bind him anymore, not even with a chain. For he had often been chained hand and foot, but he tore the chains apart and broke the irons on his feet. No one was strong enough to subdue him. Night and day among the tombs and in the hills he would cry out and cut himself with stones.

"When he saw Yeshua from a distance, he ran and fell on his knees in front of him. He shouted at the top of his voice, 'What do you want with me, Yeshua, Son of the Most High God? In God's name don't torture me!' For Yeshua had said to him, 'Come out of this man, you impure spirit!'

"Then Yeshua asked him, 'What is your name?'

"'My name is Legion,' he replied, 'for we are many.' And he begged Yeshua again and again not to send them out of the area.

"A large herd of pigs was feeding on the nearby hillside. The demons begged Yeshua, 'Send us among the pigs; allow us to go into them.' He gave them permission, and the impure spirits came out and went into the pigs. The herd, about two thousand in number, rushed down the steep bank into the lake and were drowned.

"Those tending the pigs ran off and reported this in the town and countryside, and the people went out to see what had happened. When they came to Yeshua, they saw the man who had been possessed by the legion of demons, sitting there, dressed and in his right mind; and they were afraid. Those who had seen it told the people what had happened to the demon-possessed man—and told about the pigs as well. Then the people began to plead with Yeshua to leave their region.

"As Yeshua was getting into the boat, the man who had been demon-possessed begged to go with him. Yeshua did not let him, but said, 'Go home to your own people and tell them how much the Lord has done for you, and how he has had mercy on you.' So the man went away and began to tell in the Decapolis how much Yeshua had done for him. And all the people were amazed." [Mark 5]

Do you have any idea what it's like to be completely ostracized from your own people and village, to regularly lose awareness of where you are or what's happening, to occasionally have a moment of lucidity and find yourself chained up in graveyard and then finally someone comes to help from a completely unexpected quarter? Not family, not friends, not fellow residents of your village, not a local physician, nor an astrologer, nor a sage. Not anyone you'd ever heard of before. That in fact is my story. I was not seeking Yeshua, or looking for him, or expecting him to eventually show up where I was, it came entirely as a surprise. I guess that is what is meant by "grace"—unexpected, undeserved, unmerited benefit or blessing.

Demon possession is a horrible thing because you lose control of yourself. The demonic forces take over the center of your being, your very heart, and you are helpless, being in thrall to them. And in my case, it was not just one demon, but many. Yeshua later told me that they called themselves "legion" like a Roman military unit. Whatever they were, I was a completely conquered and crushed victim of their malevolence. And when Yeshua exorcised them from inside of me, I am told that something happened that made his Jewish followers with him laugh. We have swine herders around here, but there are none in Galilee because pig meat is forbidden for a Jew to eat. The Jews also have a term for demons, they call them unclean spirits. So in my case, the unclean spirits requested to enter unclean animals who then ran pell-mell into the sea.

For a Jew, this was a perfect outcome—two forms of uncleanness destroyed at once! But for my people, it was a disaster, various herders losing their means of living. This is why the people in the area, even after they saw that I was whole again, a sane person again, asked Yeshua to leave the area, and he promptly did. I wish I had followed him, in spite of what he told me to do, but there was something about his authoritative presence. When he told you to do something, it felt like he was empowering you to do it, and you did not want to disappoint him. I hear that Yeshua exorcised various other demons on the other side of the lake as well. It seems the Jews have the same problems we have. Perhaps the powers of darkness have met their match at last. I lost track of the man a long time ago, but I have not forgotten him. He changed my life for the better, and helped return me to my people. I will not stop remembering him and telling people about him until the day I pass away.

CHAPTER TEN

THE SYROPHOENECIAN WOMAN

CALL ME THE CANAANITE WOMAN. I AM FROM THE REGION OF TYRE AND
Sidon, now part of the Syrian province of the Roman Empire. The Romans
call the region Syro-Phoenicia as opposed to Labo-Phoenicia, a colony of
the Phoenicians on the north coast of Africa. I am not a Jew, but I had heard
of the healer called Yeshua. Imagine my surprise when he showed up in my
very region exactly at the time when my daughter desperately needed his
help. I myself was desperate, and prepared to do most anything to get her
help, including falling on my knees and begging the healer to act. She was
my only child, and my husband had left me long ago. I had no one else in
my life, no one else to love or care for, no one who loved me. Here are two
different accounts of my encounter with Yeshua.

"*Leaving that place, Yeshua withdrew to the region of Tyre and Sidon.
A Canaanite woman from that vicinity came to him, crying out, 'Lord, Son*

of David, have mercy on me! My daughter is demon-possessed and suffering terribly.'

"Yeshua *did not answer a word. So his disciples came to him and urged him,* 'Send her away, for she keeps crying out after us.'

"He answered, *'I was sent only to the lost sheep of Israel.'*

"The woman came and knelt before him. 'Lord, help me!' she said.

"He replied, 'It is not right to take the children's bread and toss it to the dogs.'

"'Yes it is, Lord,' she said. 'Even the dogs eat the crumbs that fall from their master's table.'

"Then Yeshua said to her, 'Woman, you have great faith! Your request is granted.' And her daughter was healed at that moment." [Matthew 15]

"Yeshua left that place and went to the vicinity of Tyre. He entered a house and did not want anyone to know it; yet he could not keep his presence secret. In fact, as soon as she heard about him, a woman whose little daughter was possessed by an impure spirit came and fell at his feet. The woman was a Greek, born in Syrian Phoenicia. She begged Yeshua to drive the demon out of her daughter.

"'First let the children eat all they want,' he told her, 'for it is not right to take the children's bread and toss it to the dogs.'

"'Lord,' she replied, 'even the dogs under the table eat the children's crumbs.'

"Then he told her, 'For such a reply, you may go; the demon has left your daughter.'

"She went home and found her child lying on the bed, and the demon gone." [Mark 7]

One of the things that strikes me most, at this great remove in time is that when you hear or read a report like this, it is impossible to discern the tone with which certain things are sometimes said. I have come to the conclusion that Yeshua was not trying to be abrupt or stern with me, he was testing me, and perhaps his disciples as well who had urged him to send me away. I knew he was sent to his fellow Jews, but he was not close-minded about helping others. Indeed, to this day I have wondered why in the world he was near Tyre and Sidon. Was he simply trying to get away from the crowds in Galilee for a while? I don't know.

No question but the disciples were annoyed with me, and perhaps that was in part because they too wanted to get away from the crowds wanting healing from Yeshua. They wanted Yeshua to send me away, but instead of doing that, he engaged me in a challenging conversation.

You may ask—"Did he really call you a dog?" Dog has always been a slur used by Jews and others about foreign women? Well, not directly. He was using an illustration involving children and dogs, and of course few if any people in my world have dogs in the house as pets. Dogs are scavengers, mongrels in my world. Sometimes they would dart into the open front doorway of a house, which especially in the summer is normally left open so there can be a chance of a little breeze coming into the house. They would scamper in and grab some morsel from under one of the dining couches or small tables and run off. The poor creatures need to eat after all. I took Yeshua's stern words as a test, because I detected no malice in his tone. He was pushing me to see what I would say, to see if I would exhibit perseverance and faith.

I do not remember how I came up with my response, but I accepted his judgment that his fellow Jews had first claim on his help, but there was still a way he could help others as well. But when he exclaimed—"Woman you have great faith!" I felt something good was about to happen, and sure enough, it did. But he made me exhibit my faith, as I had to trust what he said had or would happen for my little girl was true.

So I mustered up my courage, went home, and there she was, lying on her little cot, a smile on her face, and in her right mind. I fell to my knees and thanked whatever G-d had just helped me. The light of my life was shining bright again, and I had hope for the future. I never saw Yeshua again. Some years later, I met some of his followers in Sidon. They claimed that though he died, he had risen again from the dead and ascended into the heavens. Who am I to dispute this claim? A man who can cast out demons from a little girl, without so much as seeing her or touching her is capable of all kinds of things. For my part, I am thankful for the day I happened to encounter Yeshua. I still wonder if it was just a chance encounter, or something more like divine providence. Perhaps someday I will know for sure.

CHAPTER ELEVEN

THE CENTURION'S SERVANT

I AM A MAN UNDER AUTHORITY, AND I KNOW HOW TO TAKE ORDERS FROM my superiors. I have also been a man in authority who knows how to give orders. But when you are dealing with someone who has some kind of direct divine authority and power, you realize you cannot order such a person to do this or that. You have to approach them carefully, with honor and respect, and make a request.

Let me back up and tell you the story. I am in a Roman auxiliary unit, based in Capernaum, a small village by the sea of Tiberias. I am not a Roman myself, but rather a native of this very region, who joined the Roman army to feed my family. Originally my legion was based in Syria, but when Judea became a Roman province as well, some of us moved into Galilee, especially after the insurrections led by Judas the Galilean due to the census under Quirinius some eight or so years after Herod the Great had died.

Over the course of my living in Capernaum I began to attend the synagogue there, and felt it would be a good "liturgy," my civic service, if I supported this synagogue financially and help with its further construction. I have become what the Jews call a G-d-fearer. I have found real comfort that there is just one real deity, one real knowable god, to whom one may pray and expect succor and aid. And believe me I was praying hard because my best servant, the one I had plans to manumit and make my son and heir, was deathly ill.

It was at this juncture that the synagogue elders came to me and had a suggestion of who might be able to help. They had seen him heal a paralytic right in the synagogue during the Sabbath service in Capernaum. I had been away on duty doing surveillance with my troops when that happened. Later, one of the synagogue elders managed to procure a report written down by some follower of Yeshua about what happened on that most blessed of all days when Yeshua came to town. This is what it said—

"*Now when Yeshua concluded all His sayings in the hearing of the people, He entered Capernaum. And a certain centurion's servant, who was dear to him, was sick and ready to die. So when he heard about Yeshua, he sent elders of the Jews to Him, pleading with Him to come and heal his servant. And when they came to Yeshua, they begged Him earnestly, saying that the one for whom He should do this was deserving, 'for he loves our nation, and has built us a synagogue.'*

"*Then Yeshua went with them. And when He was already not far from the house, the centurion sent friends to Him, saying to Him, 'Lord, do not trouble Yourself, for I am not worthy that You should enter under my roof. Therefore I did not even think myself worthy to come to You. But say the word, and my servant will be healed, for I also am a man placed under authority, having soldiers under me. And I say to one, "Go," and he goes; and to another, "Come," and he comes; and to my servant, "Do this," and he does it.'*

"*When Yeshua heard these things, He marveled at him, and turned around and said to the crowd that followed Him, 'I say to you, I have not found such great faith, not even in Israel!' And those who were sent, returning to the house, found the servant well who had been sick.*" [Matthew 8, cf. John 4]

Faith is many things, but what I took Yeshua to mean was that trusting someone means taking them at their word, something we soldiers have to do. When our commander says, "We are about to be attacked, and if we don't move now, we will be in peril," we take him at his word, trusting that he is telling the truth. I knew Yeshua to be a man of great power and authority, and also an honest man, a truth teller. It was then not difficult for me to say what I did, trusting he would respond. When I got back to my house my servant was already well.

These were early days in Yeshua's ministry, long before he fell afoul of Pilate in Judea. He already had a reputation as a healer, and I had no reason to doubt it was so. I had seen all kinds of signs and wonders and marvels in my day. In Galilee there was a long tradition of miracle workers, going back to prophetic figures like Elijah and Elisha, whom I had learned about in the synagogue. The Galileans were proud of this 'northern' prophetic tradition as they called it, and there had been much talk about of it in light of John the Baptizer who dressed and talked like Elijah, and the rumor was he might be the latter-day Elijah figure who comes before judgment day. Sometime after Yeshua healed my servant I learned he was the cousin of John. I must confess that I find all of this confusing. We are now on the cusp of a major war here in Galilee. Both Yeshua and John talked about coming judgment and it seems to be imminent since I hear Vespasian is on the way with several more legions, but Yeshua also proclaimed good news of salvation for G-d's people. Romans talk about peace after victory, perhaps there will be salvation after pacification? But I am only hoping and guessing. What I am more sure about is that Yeshua was what he seemed to be. He was no false prophet, or make-believe messiah, or charlatan pretending to be a healer. Take that for what you will.

CHAPTER TWELVE

THE WIDOW OF NAIN

NAIN HARDLY QUALIFIES AS A TOWN, IT'S SO SMALL. AND HERE, EVERYONE knows everyone else's business. So when my son died, the whole village came out for the funeral. Let me just say that no parent wants to outlive their children. It is hard enough losing a child at all, but especially hard when you are old, and there is no more prospect of children, not just because you are old, but because your husband has been gathered to his ancestors some time ago.

During that week of mourning, I was inconsolable. My only begotten son was dead. How had it happened? One moment he seemed fine. The next he simply fell over in his chair, quivered for a moment, and then gave up his spirit. One moment we were laughing and having our normal meal together. The next moment he was gone. I was in such shock, I hardly even cried out. When it first happened I prayed hard for G-d to reverse the

outcome. I had never prayed so hard in my life. I got on my knees and literally begged G-d to intervene. Little did I know then that my prayers would
be answered, but not in the way I expected. I have learned that G-d answers
prayer not on the basis of our request, but on the basis of our need. And my
need had just become great. I had no one to support me in my old age, and
I might even lose what I had, since there was no male heir. I was forlorn,
angry, and alone—so very alone.

A man named Luke passed through here some time ago, collecting
stories of Yeshua, whom I knew was from nearby Nazareth. I knew him
of course by reputation. Everyone had heard the stories about stupendous
miracles. I was not sure what to make of them. Here is how Luke tells the
story of the best day in my life . . .

*"Soon afterward, Yeshua went to a town called Nain, and his disciples
and a large crowd went along with him. As he approached the town gate, a
dead person was being carried out—the only son of his mother, and she was
a widow. And a large crowd from the town was with her. When the Lord saw
her, his heart went out to her and he said, 'Don't cry.'*

*"Then he went up and touched the bier they were carrying him on, and
the bearers stood still. He said, 'Young man, I say to you, get up!' The dead
man sat up and began to talk, and Yeshua gave him back to his mother. They
were all filled with awe and praised G-d. 'A great prophet has appeared among
us,' they said. 'G-d has come to help his people.' This news about Yeshua spread
throughout Judea and the surrounding country.* [Luke 7]

I am still dumbfounded by that day. I had never seen anything like
that in my many years before, and nothing since then either. I guess that's
the very nature of a miracle—it's rare, rare and precious. Unlooked for, unexpected, but also undeniable. My son had been dead for more than a day,
and then the oddest thing ever happened.

I had heard the stories of Elijah raising a dead child, but it had not really penetrated my thinking that G-d still did those kinds of things through
his prophets. Yeshua came to our village right during the funeral procession. It was somber and solemn and sad. He was a man who had such a
presence, such innate authority, but he interrupted the funeral procession
and came directly to me and said quietly, "Don't cry." That's all he said, but I
could see the tears glistening in his own eyes which seemed so odd. He told
me not to cry and there he was weeping with me.

The second odd thing was that he went over and touched the funeral
bier. No one does that except the pallbearers, not least because of the

concern about corpse uncleanness, which lasts for seven days. Yet Yeshua was not in the least concerned about how things would affect him. He was concerned about how it had affected me! Me, a widow! Me, a nobody of no repute! Me, a person that even Luke the storyteller did not mention by name. He only said I was a widow.

Immediately the pallbearers stopped the procession when Yeshua touched the bier, and then a further truly strange thing happened—Yeshua addressed the corpse as if it were still alive, still could hear!

My son shot straight up, as if he had been suddenly awakened by a shout, or a clap of thunder and he began to talk, and talk, and talk, as if nothing had happened to him. Later he told me how very strange it felt to find himself wrapped in a winding sheet on a bier.

I shook. When I saw this I shook. You know we pray and pray, and then we are shocked when G-d actually answers a prayer in the affirmative. I lost control of myself. I felt faint, but leaned on my cane and avoided falling down. The next thing I knew, Yeshua was handing me back my boy! And what a glad heart I had then! You cannot imagine the exhilaration I felt.

The townspeople were only a little less amazed than me. They began shouting praises to our G-d. They spoke of having been visited by a great prophet, like another northern prophet of old, Elijah no doubt. Indeed, the word about this spread all the way to Judea. And speaking of Judea, I felt the need to do something to thank G-d for this miracle. I don't have much, but I determined on that day I would go up to Jerusalem and make an offering to G-d. The strange thing is—without intending to do so, I ran into Yeshua again! Here is the story as Luke told it:

As Yeshua looked up, he saw the rich putting their gifts into the temple treasury. He also saw a poor widow put in two very small copper coins. 'Truly I tell you,' he said, 'this poor widow has put in more than all the others. All these people gave their gifts out of their wealth; but she out of her poverty put in all she had to live on.'" [Luke 21]

It was what was left of my dowry. Since I had my son to provide for me and look after me, I felt I could give all the coins I had left as a thank offering. I never expected Yeshua to use the instance as a teaching moment, but he did. I was so glad to see him one final time. He would be dead before that week was over. And he was so full of life then, so animated. I will never understand why the authorities felt they had to do away with him. He was a great man of G-d, a great prophet, a great healer, and a man of a very large heart. I am still haunted by the time he looked directly into my eyes and whispered—"Don't cry." I will hear the sweet sound of that voice of compassion speaking into my darkness until the day I die. He changed my life for the better. The least I could do was go on pilgrimage and make a thank offering to G-d.

CHAPTER THIRTEEN

BAR TIMAEUS

YOU DON'T EVEN KNOW MY NAME. IT'S NOT BARTIMAEUS, I CAN TELL YOU that. That's just a patronymic that means "son of Timaeus." Timaeus was my father, not me. He was not blind, that was me! He was not a beggar on the side of the road near ancient Jericho, that was me! If I sound bitter . . . well I have been. How would you like to live in darkness for years and years of your life, to not be able to have or support a family, to have to sit on the side of the road with a beggar's bowl hoping for acts of compassion and charity? Mind you, I'm less bitter now, but there still is a bit of that in me.

Then there came a day when I heard about Yeshua through the chattering of the crowds passing me on the way up to Jerusalem, for I was sitting on the main road from Jericho to Jerusalem where the pilgrims all had to pass. This location was good for me because not only did a lot of people pass me and give a coin or two, but also since they were going up to festival many felt more obliged to give alms as they sought to do their religious duties in Jerusalem. In other words, I was in the perfect spot to move them to charity if they were ever to be so moved. But then the word came that Yeshua was on his way, and there was great excitement. As it turned out, there was huge crowd of disciples and onlookers simply traveling with him. I had already heard from my friend Zaccheus who lives in Jericho what Yeshua could do for a person, and so I was excited to hear that he was passing through town again. Here is how a later follower of Yeshua told my tale.

"*Then they came to Jericho. As Yeshua and his disciples, together with a large crowd, were leaving the city, a blind man, Bartimaeus (which means 'son of Timaeus'), was sitting by the roadside begging. When he heard that it was Yeshua of Nazareth, he began to shout, 'Yeshua, Son of David, have mercy on me!'*

"*Many rebuked him and told him to be quiet, but he shouted all the more, 'Son of David, have mercy on me!'*

"*Yeshua stopped and said, 'Call him.'*

"*So they called to the blind man, 'Cheer up! On your feet! He's calling you.' Throwing his cloak aside, he jumped to his feet and came to Yeshua.*

"'*What do you want me to do for you?' Yeshua asked him.*

"*The blind man said, 'Rabbi, I want to see.'*

"'*Go,' said Yeshua, 'your faith has healed you.' Immediately he received his sight and followed Yeshua along the road.*" [Mark 10]

When Yeshua drew near he was being talked to by lots of people, and many were pressing up against him. The noise was incredible, as was the excitement. Some were singing the Hallel psalms—"Let's go up to Zion, let's go up to Zion, the city of the great King," songs pilgrims sing on the way to Jerusalem. Some were talking about miracles Yeshua had performed in Galilee. I grew frantic, fearing he would pass and not see me, so I cried out "Son of David."

The reason I cried out that way is because *the* son of David was of course Solomon, and he was famous for his wisdom, including wisdom to cure people of things. Yeshua, in my mind, seemed like him—he was a wise rabbi and a healer. So I called him Son of David. And I pleaded for mercy. Some fool tried to silence me, rebuked me, telling me to shut up. But I was not going to miss my chance. So I shouted again. This time Yeshua heard me and stopped along the dust road. He told one of his disciples to call me, and one of them told me to be of good cheer because the Master was calling for me. I suddenly felt hope and anticipation in my heart, and my pulse quickened.

He didn't come to me, he wanted me to come to him. Picture me suddenly standing up, with my walking stick and groping my way towards the sound of Yeshua's voice. I threw off my outer cloak, which encumbered me, so I could walk more freely, and shuffled slowly, carefully in the right direction.

Now it was perfectly clear that I could not see. And anyone who knows the Scriptures knows there is no story there about the healing of a man who is blind. Isaiah promises this will happen someday, but there's no recorded incident of it in days of old. Still, I thought—maybe Isaiah's word will be fulfilled today. I was surprised when Yeshua asked what I wanted him to do for me, but I was not going to be put off. Later I figured out he wanted me to participate in my own healing, which is why I was asked to come to him. I told him in my plaintive little voice that was cracking with emotion, "Please sir, I would like to see for the first time."

He never touched me. He never laid a hand on me. All he did was say, "Go, your faith has healed you." Suddenly, light broke through into my life. I had to shield my eyes it was so bright, but I wanted the first sight I saw to be my healer—Yeshua, so I followed him on the way to Jerusalem. And why not. I had much to be thankful for. I began to sing the psalm . . .

> I cry aloud to the Lord;
>   I lift up my voice to the LORD for mercy.
> I pour out before him my complaint;
>   before him I tell my trouble.

Yeshua emphasized that it was not some magical procession or cloth that healed me, I was healed because I trusted that Yeshua could heal me. Without the faith, it would not have happened. I am sure of that. But without Yeshua, the healing was not even possible. On that day I became his follower, and continue to be so, even until now, as a very old man. I still live here in Jericho, and I tell whoever will listen what happened to me. Some believe, some do not, but none can deny I can now see. The evidence is right before them, staring them in the face!

THE SAMARITAN WOMAN

I WAS MINDING MY OWN BUSINESS, AND HOPING TO AVOID CONTACT WITH other women of the village, so I went to the well at mid-day, not at dawn as was the normal practice. My marriage history was the constant subject of cheap jokes and ridicule in my village, and it got worse when I decided to move in with a man who was not my husband. Then tongues really began to wag, but they couldn't do much because my latest partner is wealthy, a major benefactor of the synagogue, and the village knew it couldn't afford to lose his patronage. Some of them just criticized behind my back, and gossiped as always. Others went to the rabbi to get him to do something, but he didn't.

I sometimes wonder if some of these old women would have anything substantive to talk about if it were not for my tumultuous personal relationships. Of course they forget that in each case, it was a man who initiated these relationships, not me! The men came after me, not the reverse. Sometimes being a woman who is attractive is a curse, rather than a blessing, but the truth was I was not a person of independent means, so I had to have a man in my life to survive. Such is the way things work in a man's world, and let me be clear, Samaria, like Galilee, like Judea is a male-dominated society. There's nothing I could do about that. But you did not come to me to hear me complain about the nature of our broken world. You want to hear about my encounter with Yeshua. Fair enough. But since I am not an educated person, I will let one of Yeshua's later disciples tell my story for me, and then I will provide some further remarks to explain. This is how that disciple told it . . .

"So Yeshua left Judea and went back once more to Galilee. Now he had to go through Samaria. So he came to a town in Samaria called Sychar, near the plot of ground Jacob had given to his son Joseph. Jacob's well was there, and Yeshua, tired as he was from the journey, sat down by the well. It was about noon.

"When a Samaritan woman came to draw water, Yeshua said to her, 'Will you give me a drink?' (His disciples had gone into the town to buy food.)

"The Samaritan woman said to him, 'You are a Jew and I am a Samaritan woman. How can you ask me for a drink?' (For Jews do not associate with Samaritans.)

"Yeshua answered her, 'If you knew the gift of G-d and who it is that asks you for a drink, you would have asked him and he would have given you living water.'

"'Sir,' the woman said, 'you have nothing to draw with and the well is deep. Where can you get this living water? Are you greater than our father Jacob, who gave us the well and drank from it himself, as did also his sons and his livestock?'

"Yeshua answered, 'Everyone who drinks this water will be thirsty again, but whoever drinks the water I give them will never thirst. Indeed, the water I give them will become in them a spring of water welling up to eternal life.'

"The woman said to him, 'Sir, give me this water so that I won't get thirsty and have to keep coming here to draw water.'

"He told her, 'Go, call your husband and come back.'

"'I have no husband,' she replied.

"Yeshua said to her, 'You are right when you say you have no husband. The fact is, you have had five husbands, and the man you now have is not your husband. What you have just said is quite true.'

"'Sir,' the woman said, 'I can see that you are a prophet. Our ancestors worshiped on this mountain, but you Jews claim that the place where we must worship is in Jerusalem.'

"'Woman,' Yeshua replied, 'believe me, a time is coming when you will worship the Father neither on this mountain nor in Jerusalem. You Samaritans worship what you do not know; we worship what we do know, for salvation is from the Jews. Yet a time is coming and has now come when the true worshipers will worship the Father in the Spirit and in truth, for they are the kind of worshipers the Father seeks. G-d is spirit, and his worshipers must worship in the Spirit and in truth.'

"The woman said, 'I know that Messiah' (called Christ) 'is coming. When he comes, he will explain everything to us.'

Then Yeshua declared, 'I, the one speaking to you—I am he.'

"Just then his disciples returned and were surprised to find him talking with a woman. But no one asked, 'What do you want?' or 'Why are you talking with her?'

"Then, leaving her water jar, the woman went back to the town and said to the people, 'Come, see a man who told me everything I ever did. Could this be the Messiah?' They came out of the town and made their way toward him.

"Meanwhile his disciples urged him, 'Rabbi, eat something.'

"But he said to them, 'I have food to eat that you know nothing about.'

"Then his disciples said to each other, 'Could someone have brought him food?'

"'My food,' said Yeshua, 'is to do the will of him who sent me and to finish his work. Don't you have a saying, "It's still four months until harvest"? I tell you, open your eyes and look at the fields! They are ripe for harvest. Even now the one who reaps draws a wage and harvests a crop for eternal life, so that the sower and the reaper may be glad together. Thus the saying "One sows and another reaps" is true. I sent you to reap what you have not worked for. Others have done the hard work, and you have reaped the benefits of their labor.'

"Many of the Samaritans from that town believed in him because of the woman's testimony, 'He told me everything I ever did.' So when the Samaritans came to him, they urged him to stay with them, and he stayed two days. And because of his words many more became believers.

"They said to the woman, 'We no longer believe just because of what you said; now we have heard for ourselves, and we know that this man really is the Savior of the world.'" [John 4]

If you're going to understand my story, you need to know something about the antipathy between Jews and Samaritans. The story of course says we will not share a common cup, share in hospitality with one another, but that is just the first shoot of the plant coming up from the dirt below. Jews and Samaritans have been hating and killing each other for a long time. At the time of the Assyrian invasion many centuries before the time of Yeshua, some of our leaders were carted off into exile, but most of us remained. The Jews of Judea did not come and help us, and likewise when the Babylonian ruler Nebuchadnezzar came calling in Jerusalem, we did not help the Jews out. Indeed, many of our people were glad to see them go into exile.

To this day, Jews generally avoid traveling through Samaria because many of their teachers say our land is perpetually unclean, like the uncleanness of the corpse. In fact they mostly bypass Samaria if they are traveling from Galilee to Judea or the reverse. It says something about how different Yeshua was that he had no problems with being in Samaria or reaching out to Samaritans. Perhaps you will remember the little parable he told in various places, including here in Sychar when he visited for several days. This is what it says . . .

"On one occasion an expert in the law stood up to test Yeshua. 'Teacher,' he asked, 'what must I do to inherit eternal life?'

"'What is written in the Law?' he replied. 'How do you read it?'

He answered, "'Love the Lord your G-d with all your heart and with all your soul and with all your strength and with all your mind'; and, 'Love your neighbor as yourself.'"

"'You have answered correctly,' Yeshua replied. 'Do this and you will live.'

But he wanted to justify himself, so he asked Yeshua, 'And who is my neighbor?'

In reply Yeshua said: 'A man was going down from Jerusalem to Jericho, when he was attacked by robbers. They stripped him of his clothes, beat him and went away, leaving him half dead. A priest happened to be going down the same road, and when he saw the man, he passed by on the other side. So too, a Levite, when he came to the place and saw him, passed by on the other side. But a Samaritan, as he traveled, came where the man was; and when he saw him, he took pity on him. He went to him and bandaged his wounds, pouring on oil and wine. Then he put the man on his own donkey, brought him to an inn and took care of him. The next day he took out two denarii and gave them to the innkeeper. 'Look after him,' he said, 'and when I return, I will reimburse you for any extra expense you may have.'

"'Which of these three do you think was a neighbor to the man who fell into the hands of robbers?'

The expert in the law replied, 'The one who had mercy on him.'

Yeshua told him, 'Go and do likewise.'" [Luke 10]

The thing that is most notable about this parable is that Yeshua would choose a Samaritan to provide the illustration for the commandment to love neighbor as self, suggesting that any definition of neighbor that did not include Samaritans and other non-Jews, was not broad enough. Few Jewish teachers would use Samaritans as moral paradigms in their teachings. You will notice as well that the Samaritan was himself in foreign territory, and yet he went out of his way to be merciful, and show how to be a neighbor to others.

The Jews say that this parable is based on a story in their Scriptures. Their Torah is different from ours. We only believe in the books of Moses. Nothing else. But in a book sometimes called Kingdoms and sometimes called Chronicles, there is a story that may have been in Yeshua's mind [2 Chronicles 28:8–15]. In any event, I am rather sure this parable would have been offensive to most Jews. This is especially so because of what I can only call worship wars between our peoples. Let me explain.

In one of the Jewish late writings [Neh 4:1–2] we are told that both the governor of Judea appointed by Darius (a man named Sandballat) and also the "army" of Samaria were opposed to the rebuilding of the temple and the city walls in Jerusalem [cf. Ezra 4]. A little over a century later, we Samaritans did build our own temple on Mt. Gerizim, which in turn was destroyed by the Hellenized Jewish ruler John Hyrcanus some one hundred fifty years before Yeshua visited our village. These two sets of actions of course only raised the level of antipathy between Jews and Samaritans, so you can understand why I tried to steer the conversation in the direction I did. I wanted to see what Yeshua would say about *where* the true temple was. Instead, he chose to talk about *what* the true worship should be like. I had changed the subject to that discussion because Yeshua had brought up my colorful past.

Listen, a woman like me, whose background has been morally questioned would be considered truly unclean. So it was difficult for me to understand why in the world Yeshua, obviously a Jew because he was wearing a Jewish prayer shawl which we do not wear, would ask me for a cup of water. If I hand him such a cup, would he not then become unclean in his own eyes? And yet, he seemed untroubled by such questions. He was not afraid to drink from a cup I gave him, nor was he concerned about avoiding conversation with me, even a deep conversation.

We Samaritans have rather specific beliefs about what a messiah figure will be likely. Naturally, since we only believe in the five books of Moses, we expect him to be like Moses, or at least like the latter day prophet Moses spoke of in his last book who would come and reveal to us where on Mt. Gerizim were hidden the sacred vessels he left there from the tabernacle of long ago. Imagine how shocked I was when Yeshua said he was in fact this prophetic figure! But then it began to make sense because he had unveiled the secret of my life without me telling him any of my personal story! I ran to tell the people of the village, and made enough of a noise and ruckus to get them to come and meet this Yeshua. The amazing thing is that when I told them what he had said about my relationships, the very topic they so often had discussed, well, they believed he must be a prophet and so they came out to meet him. I was rather disappointed after the fact when they decided to say that they no longer believed in him because of my testimony but because they had encountered him for themselves. Typical, but disappointing.

I honestly did not know what to make of Yeshua's traveling disciples. They seemed more concerned about finding food to feed their faces, than with bringing people to benefit from the presence of Yeshua. And they seemed obtuse as well, thinking Yeshua was talking about mundane things when really he was talking about deeper things, like spiritual food and spiritual water. Yeshua seems also to have spoken to them about sowers and reapers referring to those who share the good word about Yeshua, and those who help bring people into the fold of believing in him, but as things turned out, Yeshua and I were the sowers of the Word, not those disciples.

One more thing about my exchange with Yeshua, lest you think I was dense as well. The phrase 'living water' in our world means running water. So when Yeshua first talked about living water, I thought he was talking about a stream, as opposed to a well. As it turned out, he was discussing a much deeper sort of soul-quenching water. Perhaps I shouldn't be so hard on those disciples, since I made the same mistake by thinking on the mundane level at first about the water, just as they did about the food. In any case, the outcome was that Yeshua and his disciples stayed for several more days, and one of our people even suggested as a result of this further time together that Yeshua was the savior of the world. Since he meets all the criteria we Samaritans expected, as outlined by the life and teaching of

Moses, I must say that I agree with this, as many others have done in the years since he visited among us.

ELIEZAR

NO MATTER WHAT YOU MIGHT THINK, I SHOULD NOT BE CONFUSED WITH
John Zebedee. He was a Galilean disciple, one of Yeshua's inner circle of
three. I, on the other hand, am a Judean disciple of Yeshua. I used to live in
Bethany, but now I'm in Ephesus. *It was me*, I'm the only named disciple
about whom it was said he is 'the one whom Yeshua loved.' Of course Yeshua loved all of us. Of course he did. But our relationship was especially
close. Every time Yeshua came up to the festivals in Jerusalem he stayed
with us—Martha, Miriam, and myself. We were close, like family. So you
need to understand that when I died, it was not just devastating to Miriam
and Martha, it was devastating to Yeshua as well. My sisters say he wept at
my grave. I'm sure that he did. But he intended to do something about it,
and miraculously enough—he did!

I would not be telling you all this if I had not been raised from the dead and gone on to serve the Lord both in the promised land and elsewhere. And I have written down my testimony for all to read, the testimony of the Beloved Disciple. But I am getting ahead of myself. Let's allow the testimony to speak for itself. We'll start at the dramatic point in the story and then work backwards and forwards explaining things. This part of the story is in the third person because my coworker in Ephesus, John, thought it best I let someone else tell the tale at this point, namely him. I, after all, was ill and then died and have no memory of large portions of the story at this point.

"Now a man named Eliezar was sick. He was from Bethany, the village of Miriam and her sister Martha. (This Miriam, whose brother Eliezar now lay sick, was the same one who poured perfume on the Lord and wiped his feet with her hair.) So the sisters sent word to Yeshua, 'Lord, the one you love is sick.'

"When he heard this, Yeshua said, 'This sickness will not end in death. No, it is for G-d's glory so that G-d's Son may be glorified through it.' Now Yeshua loved Martha and her sister and Eliezar. So when he heard that Eliezar was sick, he stayed where he was two more days, and then he said to his disciples, 'Let us go back to Judea.'

"'But Rabbi,' they said, 'a short while ago the Jews there tried to stone you, and yet you are going back?'

"Yeshua answered, 'Are there not twelve hours of daylight? Anyone who walks in the daytime will not stumble, for they see by this world's light. It is when a person walks at night that they stumble, for they have no light.'

"After he had said this, he went on to tell them, 'Our friend Eliezar has fallen asleep; but I am going there to wake him up.'

"His disciples replied, 'Lord, if he sleeps, he will get better.' Yeshua had been speaking of his death, but his disciples thought he meant natural sleep.

"So then he told them plainly, 'Eliezar is dead, and for your sake I am glad I was not there, so that you may believe. But let us go to him.'

"Then Thomas (also known as Didymus) said to the rest of the disciples, 'Let us also go, that we may die with him.'

"On his arrival, Yeshua found that Eliezar had already been in the tomb for four days. Now Bethany was less than two miles from Jerusalem, and many Jews had come to Martha and Miriam to comfort them in the loss of their brother. When Martha heard that Yeshua was coming, she went out to meet him, but Miriam stayed at home.

"'Lord,' Martha said to Eliezar, 'if you had been here, my brother would not have died. But I know that even now G-d will give you whatever you ask.'

"Yeshua said to her, 'Your brother will rise again.'

"Martha answered, 'I know he will rise again in the resurrection at the last day.'

"Yeshua said to her, 'I am the resurrection and the life. The one who believes in me will live, even though they die; and whoever lives by believing in me will never die. Do you believe this?'

"'Yes, Lord,' she replied, 'I believe that you are the Messiah, the Son of G-d, who is to come into the world.'

"After she had said this, she went back and called her sister Miriam aside. 'The Teacher is here,' she said, 'and is asking for you.' When Miriam heard this, she got up quickly and went to him. Now Yeshua had not yet entered the village, but was still at the place where Martha had met him. When the Jewish officials who had been with Miriam in the house, comforting her, noticed how quickly she got up and went out, they followed her, supposing she was going to the tomb to mourn there.

"When Miriam reached the place where Yeshua was and saw him, she fell at his feet and said, 'Lord, if you had been here, my brother would not have died.'

"When Yeshua saw her weeping, and the Jews who had come along with her also weeping, he was deeply moved in spirit and troubled. 'Where have you laid him?' he asked.

"'Come and see, Lord,' they replied.

"Yeshua wept.

"Then the Jewish officials said, 'See how he loved him!'

"But some of them said, 'Could not he who opened the eyes of the blind man have kept this man from dying?'

"Yeshua, once more deeply moved, came to the tomb. It was a cave with a stone laid across the entrance. 'Take away the stone,' he said.

"'But, Lord,' said Martha, the sister of the dead man, 'by this time there is a bad odor, for he has been there four days.'

"Then Yeshua said, 'Did I not tell you that if you believe, you will see the glory of G-d?'

"So they took away the stone. Then Yeshua looked up and said, 'Father, I thank you that you have heard me. I knew that you always hear me, but I said this for the benefit of the people standing here, that they may believe that you sent me.'

"When he had said this, Yeshua called in a loud voice, 'Eliezar, come out!' The dead man came out, his hands and feet wrapped with strips of linen, and a cloth around his face.

"Yeshua said to them, 'Take off the grave clothes and let him go.'

"Therefore many of the Jewish officials who had come to visit Miriam, and had seen what Yeshua did, believed in him. But some of them went to the Pharisees and told them what Yeshua had done. Then the chief priests and the Pharisees called a meeting of the Sanhedrin.

"'What are we accomplishing?' they asked. 'Here is this man performing many signs. If we let him go on like this, everyone will believe in him, and then the Romans will come and take away both our temple and our nation.'

"Then one of them, named Caiaphas, who was high priest that year, spoke up, 'You know nothing at all! You do not realize that it is better for you that one man die for the people than that the whole nation perish.'

"He did not say this on his own, but as high priest that year he prophesied that Yeshua would die for the Jewish nation, and not only for that nation but also for the scattered children of G-d, to bring them together and make them one. So from that day on they plotted to take his life.

"Therefore Yeshua no longer moved about publicly among the people of Judea. Instead he withdrew to a region near the wilderness, to a village called Ephraim, where he stayed with his disciples.

"When it was almost time for the Jewish Passover, many went up from the country to Jerusalem for their ceremonial cleansing before the Passover. They kept looking for Yeshua, and as they stood in the temple courts they asked one another, 'What do you think? Isn't he coming to the festival at all?' But the chief priests and the Pharisees had given orders that anyone who found out where Yeshua was should report it so that they might arrest him." [John 11].

Danger lurks on the horizon of this story. Yeshua was a threat to those in authority in Jerusalem. And in some ways, when Yeshua raised me from the dead, that was the straw that broke the camel's back. It precipitated the plot to get rid of Yeshua. I used to feel terrible about this, because it meant that something that happened to me was part of the cause of Yeshua's premature demise. But then I realized it was all part of G-d's plan, after all. So, let me back up and explain a few things.

Firstly, my father's name was Simon, a common name, a name that remembered what Simon Maccabee did for us, giving us our land back for a short period of time. But my father had a horrible disease. He was a leper. And of course that meant he would be shunned, and that same treatment fell on us as well. If you are wondering why three adult siblings might be still living together as adults, well it was because of what took my father from this life. We Jews are very careful about contagion, and rightly so, but it means that people who had dread diseases are necessarily isolated, even shunned. They certainly aren't marriage material. So neither Martha, nor Miriam, nor I ever married. Never. This did not mean we could not go out, go to the market, buy food, etc. Until signs of the diseases appear we would still be able to do such things. But when the skin started to turn white, and peel off . . . well, then it was over. Then we had to be avoided, at all costs. Miriam and Martha and I had been very careful, and our father had died some while ago, so we began to think we might have avoided the disease. That was until I fell ill, and the same white as snow skin started showing up, first on my hands, on my feet, on my forehead.

I remember when this happened Martha screamed, cried out to G-d that it was happening again, and to please do something. She could be very direct with G-d, and in this case she was. She yelled at Him! Well, some of the psalms were that way, so there was precedent. In any case, as soon as there were signs of serious illness, they sent off for Yeshua. He was our last best hope. I don't think Martha, to this day, understands why he delayed in coming to us, even though I explained that he had to wait for the go ahead from on high. She's still a bit upset about that delay, even all these years later.

If you were wondering why it is in that story about Martha and Miriam hosting Yeshua I am not mentioned, it's because I was away on that occasion on business. That was a year or so before I came down with my illness. But notice about the story that though Yeshua came with his disciples to Bethany, the disciples did not enter the house. They heard the tales about our father Simon, and they dared not come in for fear of contagion. Yeshua, however, had no such concerns—ever, with anyone. He was fearless about such things. He believed G-d's positive power for healing could overcome any disease or difficulty. Rather than his being contaminated by touching others, the influence went quite in the other direction—they became healed or helped by him. And he could even sense when G-d's power went forth from his involuntarily. He told me about that one time in relating the story of the woman with the blood flow.

So what happened after Yeshua had the stone rolled back and I was raised from the dead? Well, first I should say that my sisters should not be criticized for being distraught and frazzled and in shock by the time

Yeshua arrived. You would be too if that horrible feeling had set in that help had come too late to do any good. My sisters believed whole-heartedly in Yeshua, and they believed in the resurrection on the last day, but they honestly didn't expect a resurrection on the spot of one single person, namely me, hence their reaction to the request to roll back the stone. They didn't understand that Yeshua was not merely promising resurrection, he *was* the resurrection and anyone who came in contact with him could receive new life in an instant! There had never been anyone like Yeshua before. There was no precedent, the prophetic categories, even the Torah had not prepared us for who he was and what he could do.

As I was saying, after I was raised from the dead, then we had a celebratory meal in my house, and this time the disciples did come in and eat, though as you know, one of them was too critical of my sister's lavish act of devotion. I felt well, whole, and enjoyed reclining on couch with Yeshua. And we did this again early in Passover week as well in my house, the night Yeshua washed people's feet [John 13]. This was not the night of the Passover meal. That came later in the week, and within the bounds of the city of Jerusalem as was our Jewish custom. The upper room was in another house, and it would be used after Yeshua arose from the dead as well.

If you were to study closely the second half of my memoirs, you would find me mentioned at various junctures. I am the other disciple who went with Peter to Caiaphas's house when Yeshua was taken captive. They let me in the house because I was known to them by sight. Indeed, several of those Jewish officials had previously attended my funeral! Or again if you read the story of the crucifixion, none of the Twelve were present at Golgotha, but I was. I am 'the one whom Yeshua loved' and it was me to whom Yeshua bequeathed the care of his mother. She did not go back to Galilee with the Zebedees. Or again, in the story of the Sunday morning when Yeshua arose, it was I who knew where Joseph's tomb was in Jerusalem, because I, being a native of Bethany, knew the other prominent people in Jerusalem who were followers of Yeshua, some of them secretly. This is why I knew where to go to find the tomb, and Peter had to follow me. And when I saw the empty tomb, then the light dawned—what had already happened to me, had also happened to Yeshua. I did not yet know this was prophesied in Scripture, but I understood from my own experience what this empty tomb, with grave clothes neatly rolled up in the tomb, meant. Or again, if you are wondering why my memoirs don't mention a lot of the Galilean stories, indeed none of the Galilean miracles that Mark mentions except the feeding of the five thousand (and I also do not mention the Zebedees until at the very end of the chronicle), it's because my good news account focuses on the Judean and Samaritan disciples and miracles, not the Galilean ones.

It's strange how some people are. They think that because Yeshua raised me from the dead, I could never die again, or at least I would last until Yeshua returned as he promised. Yeshua did not say so, he simply told Simon "if it is my will that he remain until I return . . ." I hope the community in Ephesus finally understands this but let me explain a bit. I was raised back into my same old mortal body—still subject to disease, decay, and yes, death. I feel at this point, now almost 60 years after Yeshua was crucified, that I will be gathered to my ancestors soon, which is why I am writing down all I can remember now. I know I will die again, but I am at peace with that. It doesn't matter.

Since Yeshua is the resurrection I will continue to live with and through him, first in Paradise, and then return with him for the resurrection and the last things. That's my view. So death has no sting for me at this point. Yeshua has shown he can overcome death, over and over again, and death of course is the last and worst enemy that Satan can throw at us. If it loses its power over us, then nothing can separate us from our Lord. Nothing. Neither principalities nor powers, nor things present nor things to come. You get the point. Nothing in all of creation.

I hope you will read my chronicle someday. I have turned over my handwritten accounts of individual episodes to John now who has just returned from exile in Patmos. Thank G-d that old tyrant, Domitian is dead and the terms of exile expired. I turned it over to John because I can no longer see well, and he will form it into a good news account. I trust him to do so. And he will make clear he is just editing and sorting my various tales.

I am the Beloved Disciple, and on days I do not feel well, or feel too old, I cling to the fact Yeshua loved me as a special friend, and I will see him again. It will be like that day I walked out of the tomb and heard him say— "For goodness sake, unwrap the man, and set him free!" Someday, we will all be free, all be children of a better resurrection. In the meantime, we cling to the one who said to my sister, "I am the resurrection and the life . . ."

CHAPTER SIXTEEN

THE WOMAN CAUGHT
IN ADULTERY [1]

IT WAS A NIGHTMARE. ONE MINUTE I WAS AT THE HEIGHT OF PLEASURE with a man I cared about. The next I was being dragged out of his house kicking and screaming by the elders of the synagogue in our neighborhood. Being caught in adultery is every woman's worst nightmare if she decides to take the risk of hoping for love, over duty. You need to understand that my story is not atypical. Women are betrothed to men when they are barely

1. John 7:53—8:11 is a much beloved story, but it probably is not an original part of the Fourth Gospel. Our earliest and best manuscripts do not include it. It appears in three different places in the Fourth Gospel, and two in Luke's Gospel—A few manuscripts include these verses, wholly or in part, after John 7:36; John 21:25; Luke 21:38; or Luke 24:53. It is a story looking for a home. Nevertheless, I believe this is an authentic Yeshua story, one with a real historical basis, which is why it is included in this book. Also, see the cover of this book, the painting by Polenov of this story.

nubile—at twelve or so years of age. What do they know of love, or even sexual attraction at that age? And they have no choice but to go along with the arranged marriage. If they have domineering parents it's worse. They dare not protest. And sometimes they feel badly if they do make a minor objection, because they know that marrying the boy in question will bring needed resources to the family. It's a no-win situation. So, soon a girl barely teenager finds herself trapped. It is not rare that they are trapped in a love-less marriage, a marriage of convenience, a marriage that was little more than a property exchange!

You will say I am just justifying my bad behavior. I know well enough that what I did was wrong. I promised to be faithful . . . and I wasn't. Ours is an honor and shame culture, and the married woman's chief job, besides producing an heir, is to protect the inner life of the family, and especially protect it from the shame of sexual scandal. I failed at that. I had been married for fifteen years, no children, no love, and apparently no way out of my situation. So when an attractive unmarried young man came along, I took my chances. And I was caught, caught red-handed. Of course the way it happened wasn't at all fair. If there is a woman caught in adultery, there is also a man caught in adultery, but the elders didn't care about being fair. They heard about the story of my infidelity and they caught me.

There was a custom among the Jews that when someone sees some-thing like adultery happening they are supposed to shout out and warn those caught on the first occasion, and only take action if it happens again, because the penalty for adultery was severe—it could be stoning, it was loss of life. Well, in my case there was no warning. I was simply dragged off, I knew not where, and suddenly I found myself thrown in front of a Galilean prophet named Yeshua. I had heard of him by word of mouth, but that was all. What I knew of prophets, like John, is they were constantly thundering condemnation, so I quickly resigned myself to the worst. But shockingly, it didn't turn out that way. No it didn't. Here is how the story was later told among the disciples of Yeshua.

"*At dawn he appeared again in the temple courts, where all the people gathered around him, and he sat down to teach them. The teachers of the law and the Pharisees brought in a woman caught in adultery. They made her stand before the group and said to Yeshua, 'Teacher, this woman was caught in the act of adultery. In the Law Moses commanded us to stone such women. Now what do you say?' They were using this question as a trap, in order to have a basis for accusing him.*

"*But Yeshua bent down and started to write on the ground with his finger. When they kept on questioning him, he straightened up and said to them, 'Let any one of you who is without sin be the first to throw a stone at her.' Again he stooped down and wrote on the ground.*

"*At this, those who heard began to go away one at a time, the older ones first, until only Yeshua was left, with the woman still standing there. Yeshua straightened up and asked her, 'Woman, where are they? Has no one condemned you?'*

"*No one, sir,*" *she said.*

"*'Then neither do I condemn you,' Yeshua declared. 'Go now and leave your life of sin.'*" [John 7–8].

I need to explain a few things. Firstly, the elders are responsible for upholding the moral fiber of the community. When Yeshua said, "Let those without sin, cast the first stone," he didn't mean those who have never sinned anywhere, anytime in any way. He meant "Let those without sin *in this matter* cast the first stone." The elders realized the implications of what he said, and that's why they quickly left, from the eldest one to the younger ones.

As for Yeshua, he realized quickly that the elders were not interested in me really. They were just using me as a pawn to try to entrap him! If he said 'stone her' then he would lose his reputation as a compassionate leader. If he said 'don't stone her' then they would lambast Yeshua for not upholding Torah. It seemed like a no-win situation, that is, until Yeshua said . . . . "Let those without sin . . ." thereby springing the trap they had set for him, and in fact putting them in a no-win situation! It was a brilliant reversal of fortunes!

After the elders had left, there were just a few bystanders, disciples of Yeshua, and me. And I was just shaking and weeping. I was a mess. He lifted up my face and said quietly to me, "Are any of those who condemned you still here?" and when I said no, he added, "Neither do I condemn you, but go, and see that you don't sin like this again. Never!"

"In a daze, I wandered off thanking G-d for mercy. And I followed his advice after that. I went back to my husband and told him I had repented of my sins, and amazingly he, in a moment of honesty, apologized that he had been so hard on me and took me back! I did not expect that. Things have been much better ever since then. The biggest miracle of all is that I got pregnant and had his child. I had never seen him so happy as when the child was born. This really changed our lives for the better . . . but I've said too much about the aftermath.

One more thing about Yeshua. I do not know what he was writing in the sand. The storyteller doesn't say, and I do not know, because I cannot read or write. I suppose that this far removed from the event, it doesn't matter. It does suggest the man was literate, but that's not very important compared to the fact that he knew how to strike a balance of justice and mercy. That's how a lost sinner is redeemed. At least that's what I think.

CHAPTER SEVENTEEN

SIMON PETER

I HARDLY KNOW WHERE TO START. AS MARK TAKES THIS DOWN, I AM awaiting Roma's justice, or in this case injustice. They are a little dumbfounded that I actually requested crucifixion, but I have my reasons. I finally got to Roma, but not in the manner I had expected. I did not found the church here, but rather found the church long since planted here and growing, though the Jewish and gentile followers of Yeshua tended to meet separately. I was not happy about that. The churches here have survived the reprisals of Nero after the fire, and I hear, having tracked down both Paul and myself, that once they execute us, things may calm down, because there are rumors that Nero is in trouble with his people. I do not care about that. I am just thankful that I got that letter drafted through the skills of Silas to send off to those churches in Asia and Bithynia and elsewhere before my demise. When you know you are about to die, it certainly clarifies in your mind what's really important and what the priorities ought to be.

Let me start my tale by returning to the beginning—when Yeshua called me from my nets. Actually it had begun before then because I had heard him preach previously, and basically ignored him. I was not a follower of priests and prophets. I was a businessman trying to support my wife and family and make a living in the fishing trade. And I was doing rather well in that. We had a house in Bethsaida, and my mother-in-law retained her home in Capernaum so we gravitated between these two places on the northwest shore of the Kinneret, the so-called Sea of Galilee (I refuse to call it the Sea of Tiberias, as some have). This is how Luke summarized that day.

"One day as Yeshua was standing by the Lake of Gennesaret, the people were crowding around him and listening to the word of G-d. He saw at the water's edge two boats, left there by the fishermen, who were washing their nets. He got into one of the boats, the one belonging to Simon, and asked him to put out a little from shore. Then he sat down and taught the people from the boat.

"When he had finished speaking, he said to Simon, 'Put out into deep water, and let down the nets for a catch.'

"Simon answered, 'Master, we've worked hard all night and haven't caught anything. But because you say so, I will let down the nets.'

"When they had done so, they caught such a large number of fish that their nets began to break. So they signaled their partners in the other boat to come and help them, and they came and filled both boats so full that they began to sink.

"When Simon Peter saw this, he fell at Yeshua's knees and said, 'Go away from me, Lord; I am a sinful man!' For he and all his companions were astonished at the catch of fish they had taken, and so were James and John, the sons of Zebedee, Simon's partners.

"Then Yeshua said to Simon, 'Don't be afraid; from now on you will fish for people.' So they pulled their boats up on shore, left everything and followed him. [Luke 5]

I have to admit I was a little afraid of this man. He had this inherent power, even authority, and he was a mystery to me. Of course, he knew what might impress me, namely a big catch of fish, so he knew what might motivate me to actually listen to him, and follow him. I really didn't want to do that at the outset. I mean, I'm just an ordinary fisherman, a businessman. I'm not a leader of men or women. I wasn't interested in complicating my life by following a prophet, and besides I was no holy man. My instinctive reaction when I realize Yeshua had performed a miracle in my very presence, and on behalf of myself and my partners the Zebedees was to be frightened, and to tell Yeshua to leave me alone, because I was unworthy, a sinner.

Yeshua of course had the perfect rejoinder—"Don't worry, I'll make you a fisher of human beings," whatever that was supposed to mean. Whatever else it meant, it meant learning a new trade. Catching people is whole lot harder than catching fish, trust me on that.

The next thing I know, I'm kissing the wife goodbye, leaving my nets behind and going on the road with Yeshua. It was rather like a constant pilgrimage all over the promised land. One never knew what was coming next. I saw miracles—the raising of Jairus's daughter was amazing. The healing of a man born blind, the exorcism of demons from the Gerasene demoniac—that scared the living daylights out of most of us, though I am still laughing at seeing those pigs run pell-mell into the sea. Yeshua had a tendency to take us to remote places when he really wanted to reveal something to us, just for us disciples. Sometimes he took all of us, sometimes just me and the Zebedees. It depended on what he wanted to accomplish. For example there was that day at Caesarea Philippi, which is outside Galilee, in Herod Philip's territory.

Now Caesarea Philippi had been a pagan city named Banyas or Panyas, after the Greek god Pan. There were all these niches in the side of the mountain with statues of gods in them there, and a temple of Augustus had even been built there, with the city renamed after both Philip and the emperor—disgusting, but Philip was trying to gain more credibility and a higher honor rating with the ruler of the empire. There was the cave of Pan as well, which was thought to lead down to the river Styx or the river issued from there, it was never quite clear. The river Styx in Greek thought goes down to the land of the dead—Hades, and here was one of its portals. You need to know some of these things to really understand what happened with me that surprising day at Caesarea Philippi. Here's how one disciple told the story.

"When Yeshua came to the region of Caesarea Philippi, he asked his disciples, 'Who do people say the Son of Man is?'

"They replied, 'Some say John the Baptist; others say Elijah; and still others, Jeremiah or one of the prophets.'

"'But what about you?' he asked. 'Who do you say I am?'

"Simon Peter answered, 'You are the Messiah, the Son of the living God.'

"Yeshua replied, 'Blessed are you, Simon son of Jonah, for this was not revealed to you by flesh and blood, but by my Father in heaven. And I tell you that you are Peter, and on this rock I will build my community, and the gates of Hades will not overcome it. I will give you the keys of the kingdom of heaven; whatever you bind on earth will be bound in heaven, and whatever you loose on earth will be loosed in heaven.' Then he ordered his disciples not to tell anyone that he was the Messiah." [Matthew 16]

My given name is Simon. It was Yeshua who gave me a nickname— Cephas. The word is an Aramaic word, not a name, and what it means is "rock." Yeshua was engaging in a play on words when he said what he said at Caesarea Philippi. He actually used two related words, one for "rock" and one for "a shelf of rocks." Other disciples have often asked me what I thought Yeshua was driving at. I concluded, since he said this only after I made the right confession, that he was going to build his community on me and people like me who made the true confession. Of course the Greek name Peter comes from *petros* and similarly means "rock." It too was not a proper name. So if you call me Simon Peter, as Luke did, you are using a name and a nickname together—Simon rock . . . both names were a lot to live up to.

Yeshua made a promise on that day that his community would not die out. That's what I took from his saying about the gates of Hades, the land of the dead, not prevailing against it. He pointed to the cave of Pan when he said what he did. But then he talked about binding and loosing, which in our Jewish world referred normally to what commandments one was required or bound to obey, and which ones one was loosed or free from. The kingdom of heaven was the same thing as the kingdom of God, and I assumed that the keys referred to the judging of the confessions and life of obedience of those seeking entrance into God's saving realm.

Something odd though happened at the end of this occasion. First of all, Yeshua told us not to tell anyone he was the Jewish anointed one. I learned later this is because he wanted to reveal himself in his own way, and in his own good time. But then, just when all seemed to be going right, something else happened right after that—Yeshua began to tell us he was going to be killed, and I was very upset! This should not happen to God's anointed one. Things began to go downhill once Yeshua started talking about his early demise. Here's how a disciple told this part of my story . . .

"From that time on Yeshua began to explain to his disciples that he must go to Jerusalem and suffer many things at the hands of the elders, the chief priests and the teachers of the law, and that he must be killed and on the third day be raised to life.

"Peter took him aside and began to rebuke him. 'Never, Lord!' he said. 'This shall never happen to you!'

"Yeshua turned and said to Peter, 'Get behind me, Satan! You are a stumbling block to me; you do not have in mind the concerns of God, but merely human concerns.'

"Then Yeshua said to his disciples, 'Whoever wants to be my disciple must deny themselves and take up their cross and follow me. For whoever wants to save their life will lose it, but whoever loses their life for me will find it. What good will it be for someone to gain the whole world, yet forfeit their soul? Or what can anyone give in exchange for their soul? For the Son of Man is going to come in his Father's glory with his angels, and then he will reward each person according to what they have done.'" [Matthew 16]

Just when I thought I had understood Yeshua, and responded properly, the next think I know, I'm being called Satan! And all because I didn't want him to die prematurely! It was bewildering at the time. None of us really had been taught growing up that Messiah would die a violent death, much less die on a cross. We were not looking for a crucified Messiah. Most of us expected a Messiah like King David who would be a military leader, take charge of things, clean the hostile persons out of the land. But this was not Yeshua's plan or sense of his identity at all. He wanted nothing to do with causing violence, but ironically he knew he was going to suffer it. It is interesting that sometimes the least violent persons are seen as the most dangerous ones.

Caesarea Philippi was not the only place that Yeshua revealed himself and God's plan. We also went up on another mountain and had an even more mystifying experience. Later I had Mark write down my own account of what happened, so I will give you both his third-person summary and my own account.

"After six days Yeshua took Peter, James and John with him and led them up a high mountain, where they were all alone. There he was transfigured before them. His clothes became dazzling white, whiter than anyone in the world could bleach them. And there appeared before them Elijah and Moses, who were talking with Yeshua.

"Peter said to Yeshua, 'Rabbi, it is good for us to be here. Let us put up three shelters—one for you, one for Moses and one for Elijah.' (He did not know what to say, they were so frightened.)

"Then a cloud appeared and covered them, and a voice came from the cloud: 'This is my Son, whom I love. Listen to him!'

"Suddenly, when they looked around, they no longer saw anyone with them except Yeshua.

"As they were coming down the mountain, Yeshua gave them orders not to tell anyone what they had seen until the Son of Man had risen from the dead. They kept the matter to themselves, discussing what 'rising from the dead' meant.

And they asked him, 'Why do the teachers of the law say that Elijah must come first?'

"Yeshua replied, 'To be sure, Elijah does come first, and restores all things. Why then is it written that the Son of Man must suffer much and be rejected? But I tell you, Elijah has come, and they have done to him everything they wished, just as it is written about him.'" [Mark 9]

And here is my own account . . . *"For we did not follow cleverly devised stories when we told you about the coming of our Lord Yeshua the Messiah in power, but we were eyewitnesses of his majesty. He received honor and glory from G-d the Father when the voice came to him from the Majestic Glory, saying, 'This is my Son, whom I love; with him I am well pleased.' We ourselves heard this voice that came from heaven when we were with him on the sacred mountain."* [2 Peter 1]

There's a great deal I could say about these accounts. Yeshua was trying to make clear to us exactly who he was, as was G-d. Some of it we understood, some we didn't at the time, though we understand now a lot better with benefit of hindsight and the aid of the Spirit. Different people react differently to encounters with the divine or the miraculous. Some people just go silent, stand still, and their eyes get big. Me, I'm just the opposite, I starting talking, and want to be doing something to respond because the event scares me, makes me nervous and full of energy. Mark's assessment of my response was right on target, I'm ashamed to confess. I really didn't understand what was going on, having a vision of the representatives of the Law and the Prophets, and Yeshua himself in blinding white apparel. It was apparent he was someone very special, God's very Son. But what exactly did that mean? We later learned it meant that God's very presence, and power, and glory, and majesty were being revealed in and through Yeshua, such that the person who had seen Yeshua and understood him, had seen the Father, learned of his true character and will.

Yes, I have had some mountaintop experiences, but of course I wouldn't be being honest if I didn't admit I also have had some horrible experiences as well. You will remember I promised Yeshua at the Passover meal that even if everyone else abandoned him, I would never ever do that . . . And yet Yeshua knew that I would crack under pressure and he even told me on that night that I would turn around again thereafter. It is still an unhealed wound in my soul when I remember denying him three times, the last one while swearing an oath, in the courtyard of Caiaphas, the high priest. It is a terrible thing to swear to G-d that you do not know his only Son! Equally seared into my mind was that day in Galilee where Yeshua restored our relationship. Here's how the Beloved Disciple told the tale . . .

"Afterward Yeshua appeared again to his disciples, by the Sea of Galilee. It happened this way: Simon Peter, Thomas (also known as Didymus), Nathanael from Cana in Galilee, the sons of Zebedee, and two other disciples were together. 'I'm going out to fish,' Simon Peter told them, and they said, 'We'll go with you.' So they went out and got into the boat, but that night they caught nothing.

"Early in the morning, Yeshua stood on the shore, but the disciples did not realize that it was Yeshua.

"He called out to them, 'Friends, haven't you any fish?'

"'No,' they answered.

"He said, 'Throw your net on the right side of the boat and you will find some.' When they did, they were unable to haul the net in because of the large number of fish.

"Then the disciple whom Yeshua loved said to Peter, 'It is the Lord!' As soon as Simon Peter heard him say, 'It is the Lord,' he wrapped his outer garment around him (for he had taken it off) and jumped into the water. The other disciples followed in the boat, towing the net full of fish, for they were not far from shore, about a hundred yards. When they landed, they saw a fire of burning coals there with fish on it, and some bread.

"Yeshua said to them, 'Bring some of the fish you have just caught.' So Simon Peter climbed back into the boat and dragged the net ashore. It was full of large fish, 153, but even with so many the net was not torn. Yeshua said to them, 'Come and have breakfast.' None of the disciples dared ask him, 'Who are you?' They knew it was the Lord.

"Yeshua came, took the bread and gave it to them, and did the same with the fish. This was now the third time Yeshua appeared to his disciples after he was raised from the dead.

"When they had finished eating, Yeshua said to Simon Peter, 'Simon son of John, do you love me more than these?'

"'Yes, Lord,' he said, 'you know that I love you.'

"Yeshua said, 'Feed my lambs.'

"Again Yeshua said, 'Simon son of John, do you love me?'

"He answered, 'Yes, Lord, you know that I love you.'

"Yeshua said, 'Take care of my sheep.'

"The third time he said to him, 'Simon son of John, do you love me?'

"Peter was hurt because Yeshua asked him the third time, 'Do you love me?' He said, 'Lord, you know all things; you know that I love you.'

"Yeshua said, 'Feed my sheep. Very truly I tell you, when you were younger you dressed yourself and went where you wanted; but when you are old you will stretch out your hands, and someone else will dress you and lead you where you do not want to go.' Yeshua said this to indicate the kind of death by which Peter would glorify G-d. Then he said to him, 'Follow me!'"
[John 21]

I had already seen the risen Yeshua once in Jerusalem, but he had told us he would go before us into Galilee, and so I assumed we should go back there at some point. So a few days after I saw him, I went home. I mended nets, I went fishing, and my old fishing partners the Zebedees also came, as did for the first time the Beloved Disciple, Eliezar. One of the things I learned about him was he was much more spiritually perceptive than I was. He had concluded Yeshua had risen from the dead just by looking into the tomb and finding the grave clothes rolled up there. Me, I was bewildered, but then it occurred to me that since Eliezar had himself been raised from the dead, he might well think that the same thing had happened for Yeshua.

In any case, we were fishing in the Sea of Galilee and catching exactly nothing. A man was standing on the shore at some distance, and we did not recognize him, and he called us 'young men' and made the odd suggestion to cast our nets on the other side. Now that should have triggered a memory in my mind when Yeshua had said the same thing while sitting in my boat, on the day he called me away from my nets. But I was too preoccupied at the time to make this connection. Anyway, when we caught more than a boatload of fish, Eliezar yelled out, "It's the Lord," and he was right. Being the spontaneous person I was, I quickly wrapped my outer garment around me and dove straight into the water swimming to shore. You see, I wanted so badly to be reconciled with Yeshua. I had no sense of closure, just astonishment, when I first saw him in Jerusalem, and I was determined to make amends this time for my denials. Interestingly, the same thing seems to have been on Yeshua's mind as well.

When we got to shore, Yeshua had already cooked us a breakfast, so he really didn't need our fish, but he told us to bring some anyway. He didn't want us to feel ashamed that we contributed nothing to the meal, I suppose. I'd like you to understand the exchange between Yeshua and myself. It was of course originally in Aramaic, even though Eliezar wrote it down in Greek for his own listeners. Yeshua asked me, the first time if I loved him the same as I loved these other friends. I said I did, but I used the word for brotherly love, whereas Yeshua had spoken of a higher love, a divine one. Again, he asked me if I loved him with a divine love, and I responded I loved him like a brother. But actually that is not what he asked me, now was it? But the third time, he used the same term I had used, for brotherly love, and this third time, I just lost it. I told him he knew everything . . . but what he was really probing was whether I was going to love him with all my heart, soul, mind and strength—with everything I had and serve him that way too. Was I really prepared to take up my own cross, be totally self-sacrificial, and follow him? That's what he really wanted to know, and at the end of the conversation he reminded me that indeed, I would one day be taken prisoner, bound, and hauled off for execution by the Romans, just like him. Well now, it has happened.

One thing I especially noted about the occasion was the charcoal fire. It reminded me of the one in Caiaphas's courtyard. But then I suspect Yeshua intended that, as he was going to reconfirm my commitment three times, just as I had denied him three times. And he gave me a threefold commission—to feed and tend his little lambs, his young followers, and to feed his older sheep as well. Well, I got the letter done just now and sent it off to them. I hope it helps. It talks a good deal about Yeshua being the suffering servant [see 1 Peter], and so he was. But he was after all so much more than that. G-d's yes to life in him was louder than death's no. He is the risen and reigning Lord. Thanks be to G-d.

CHAPTER EIGHTEEN

THE MOTHER OF YESHUA

THERE IS JUST TOO MUCH TO TELL, AND WHERE IN THE WORLD SHOULD I start? I could of course tell you about the angel who frightened me to death while I was only a young teenager, telling me I would be the mother of Yeshua, but without the aid of Joseph, the artisan I was betrothed to. Somehow, we survived that dangerous miracle, which could have led me to being stoned for pregnancy outside of the relationship with my husband-to-be. It was indeed a good thing we got out of Nazareth before the baby came, which is one reason I insisted on going along with Joseph to register for the census. I had not thought about the prophecy in Micah about the birth of the messiah in Bethlehem, but G-d was steering us in the right direction, whether we fully realized it or not.

There was just as much peril however after the birth, because Herod would brook no rivals, so we fled to Egypt, so often the refuge for Jews, until Herod died. Then we finally returned to Nazareth. By that point in time, the gossip had died down about my pregnancy, and we were able to get on with our married life. Joseph was a good artisan, in both stone and wood, and was in much demand, especially at that building site over the hill in Sepphoris where Herod Antipas was building a new city. The boys learned their trade there as well, especially Yeshua.

I remember vividly when Yeshua was twelve, and we went up to the festival, and already he was precocious and had lots of questions. Luke, Paul's companion, later asked me about what happened on that trip. He had heard about the mishap whereby we left Jerusalem without Yeshua. Here is how he retells the tale . . .

"Every year Yeshua's parents went to Jerusalem for the Festival of the Passover. When he was twelve years old, they went up to the festival, according to the custom. After the festival was over, while his parents were returning home, the boy Yeshua stayed behind in Jerusalem, but they were unaware of it. Thinking he was in their company, they traveled on for a day. Then they began looking for him among their relatives and friends. When they did not find him, they went back to Jerusalem to look for him. After three days they found him in the temple courts, sitting among the teachers, listening to them and asking them questions. Everyone who heard him was amazed at his understanding and his answers. When his parents saw him, they were astonished. His mother said to him, 'Son, why have you treated us like this? Your father and I have been anxiously searching for you.'

"'Why were you searching for me?' he asked. 'Didn't you know I had to be in my Father's house?' But they did not understand what he was saying to them.

"Then he went down to Nazareth with them and was obedient to them. But his mother treasured all these things in her heart. And Yeshua grew in wisdom and stature, and in favor with G-d and man." [Luke 2]

A few things need to be said about this occurrence. First of all, we traveled with relatives and friends, and it was normal for Yeshua to spend some time on the trip visiting with others. He was after all a grown boy, and quite bright. We trusted him. So when our caravan of pilgrims decided to head back to Nazareth, we assumed he knew we were all leaving, and that he would come as well. We are good parents, and not neglectful of our duties to our children. But when we discovered Yeshua was not among the Nazarene pilgrims, we became frantic. We raced back to Jerusalem and searched everywhere, finally finding him in the temple courts arguing fine points of Torah with the Torah scholars. We were shocked, to say the least, to hear all that was coming out of his mouth.

I interrupted and asked why he had treated his father and I this way. His response seemed a little like a rebuke. I had spoken of Joseph as his father, but then Yeshua said 'didn't you know I had to be in *my* Father's house?' Not the house in Nazareth, rather the holy temple in Jerusalem! Joseph did not take this well. He had so graciously accepted Yeshua as his first child, even though he was not the birth father. But before we could say any more, Yeshua quietly agreed to come home with us and was obedient to us. In truth, we really didn't understand the full significance of what he had said to us that day, but one thing we knew—he was growing in wisdom, and impressing those around him who were learned in the Scriptures, and God's favor seemed to be upon him even at twelve.

I will not recount all the years between then and when Yeshua began his ministry at about 30 years of age. They were in some ways good years, and in some ways hard years. Joseph and I had several children, both boys and girls, during that time, the first of which was Jacob. Then disaster struck, when Joseph was killed on the work site at Sepphoris, and Yeshua very ably stepped in to be the head of the family. And this is what made his departure to do ministry so difficult. He was leaving things in the hands of Jacob, whether he was ready or not, and Jacob had no high opinion of Yeshua's calling [see John 7:5]. He knew of course Yeshua could do remarkable things, but he felt Yeshua was abandoning his family when he set out to call disciples. None of my other children became his disciple before he rose from the dead. That is the sad truth of things. But let us talk of happier times, like the day that Yeshua blessed a wedding in Cana, near Nazareth. Here is how Eliezar tells the story which I once related to him . . .

"On the third day a wedding took place at Cana in Galilee. Yeshua's mother was there, and Yeshua and his disciples had also been invited to the wedding. When the wine was gone, Yeshua's mother said to him, 'They have no more wine.'

"'Woman, why do you involve me?' Yeshua replied. 'My hour has not yet come.'

"His mother said to the servants, 'Do whatever he tells you.'

"Nearby stood six stone water jars, the kind used by the Jews for ceremonial washing, each holding from twenty to thirty gallons.

"Yeshua said to the servants, 'Fill the jars with water'; so they filled them to the brim.

"Then he told them, 'Now draw some out and take it to the master of the banquet.'

"They did so, and the master of the banquet tasted the water that had been turned into wine. He did not realize where it had come from, though the servants who had drawn the water knew. Then he called the bridegroom aside and said, 'Everyone brings out the choice wine first and then the cheaper wine after the guests have had too much to drink; but you have saved the best till now.'

"'What Yeshua did here in Cana of Galilee was the first of the signs through which he revealed his glory; and his disciples believed in him.

"After this he went down to Capernaum with his mother and brothers and his disciples. There they stayed for a few days." [John 2]

This was a family wedding, not that far from where we lived in Nazareth. One of our cousins was getting married, and naturally the family was all invited. These celebrations can go on for several days, and so it is always possible to run out of food or wine. I felt we had a responsibility to help when this happened, since hospitality is such an important value in our world. This is why I appealed to Yeshua. I knew he could help. I'd seen him do remarkable things before. What I had not taken into account was that he did not want to reveal himself to others except according to the guidance of the heavenly Father, whom he called Abba. It was not his hour to fully reveal who he was and what he could do.

At first I took his "Woman, what is that to you and to me" to be a sort of rebuke, suggesting I was imposing and being presumptuous. But his tone of voice didn't suggest he would do nothing, he just wasn't going to act publicly. So I told the servants at the wedding, "Do whatever he tells you," as I was pretty sure he would try to help in an unobtrusive way. So he goes to the servants and tells them to fill up the stone purification jars with water. This may have seemed an odd request on the face of it, but the servants obeyed and did so. Then he told one of them to take a ladle and dip into one of the jars and pour it into a glass. When he did so, the water turned red! The servant was shocked, but he was the only one who knew something amazing had happened, in addition of course to me and Yeshua and his disciples, and a few family members.

It was almost funny when the toastmaster tasted the wine before speaking to the groom, and then got this peculiar look on his face—"Protocol," he said, "is you serve the best wine first, when the drinkers still have a discriminating pallet. Afterwards, you water the wine down as you go, so no one gets really drunk, and starts behaving inappropriately at the wedding. But you, you have saved the best wine until last!"

I looked at Yeshua, and he had this big grin on his face, though the wedding party and the vast majority of guests were mystified because it had been announced that the wine had run out. And so the honor of the host family was saved thanks to Yeshua. I certainly was proud of him, and he certainly was not doing anything that would have led to lots of attention focused on him. But his disciples and I knew what we knew, and we went down with him to Capernaum, having gotten a little glimpse of his coming glory. I wish I could say things stayed on this sort of positive note going forward, but soon there would be all kinds of dark questions asked about Yeshua because he started performing exorcisms all over the place, and some of his detractors began to suggest he was in league with Satan, the Wicked One.

This distressed me, and Jacob and the other children a lot, and yet Yeshua was not going to stop healing people, not going to stop the exorcisms just because of criticism. What mattered to him was that people were cured. Jacob, however, at one point articulated what several of the family members had been thinking—"He's become unbalanced. He's dabbling with darkness. Surely there is some force to the criticisms labeled at him, we need to go and rescue him, otherwise the whole family will be shamed. All of us." I had to admit, I had been worried. So we went out, with a disastrous outcome, as narrated later by Mark.

"*When his family heard about this, they went to take charge of him, for they said, 'He is out of his mind.'*

"*And the teachers of the law who came down from Jerusalem said, 'He is possessed by Beelzebul! By the prince of demons he is driving out demons.'*

"*So Yeshua called them over to him and began to speak to them in parables: 'How can Satan drive out Satan? If a kingdom is divided against itself, that kingdom cannot stand. If a house is divided against itself, that house cannot stand. And if Satan opposes himself and is divided, he cannot stand; his end has come. In fact, no one can enter a strong man's house without first tying him up. Then he can plunder the strong man's house. Amen I say to you, people can be forgiven all their sins and every slander they utter, but whoever blasphemes against the Holy Spirit will never be forgiven; they are guilty of an eternal sin.'*

"*He said this because they were saying, 'He has an impure spirit.'*

"Then Yeshua's mother and brothers arrived. Standing outside, they sent someone in to call him. A crowd was sitting around him, and they told him, 'Your mother and brothers are outside looking for you.'

"'Who are my mother and my brothers?' he asked.

"Then he looked at those seated in a circle around him and said, 'Here are my mother and my brothers! Whoever does God's will is my brother and sister and mother.'" [Mark 3]

I have to tell you that this last pronouncement felt like a slap in the face. I realized much later that what Yeshua was saying was that the family of faith was his primary family. He was not simply repudiating us, but later he invited me to join that family of faith when he said, "Woman, behold your son" from the cross. I did not understand at the time that with God's saving reigning coming, this changed the whole nature of family and indeed what priorities we must have, if we wanted to be part of what Yeshua was doing in our midst. These lessons however were hard won, and we did not really understand them until later. It took Yeshua rising from the dead before Jacob and some of the other children were prepared to really become his followers. But that day, when Yeshua would not come home with us, unlike when he was twelve, I had this sinking feeling in my heart that he was heading down a dark and dangerous road, and I could not help him, except to pray for him. He was not coming home again. Well, he did once, but it didn't go any better than the day I just described. Mark chronicled that event too. Here is what he said . . .

"Yeshua left there and went to his hometown, accompanied by his disciples. When the Sabbath came, he began to teach in the synagogue, and many who heard him were amazed.

"'Where did this man get these things?' they asked. 'What's this wisdom that has been given him? What are these remarkable miracles he is performing? Isn't this the artisan?[1] *Isn't this Miriam's son and the brother of James, Joseph, Judas and Simon? Aren't his sisters here with us?' And they took offense at him.*

"Yeshua said to them, 'A prophet is not without honor except in his own town, among his relatives and in his own home.' He could not do any miracles there, except lay his hands on a few sick people and heal them. He was amazed at their lack of faith.'" [Mark 6; cf. Luke 4]

---

1. The Greek word *tekton* does not refer specifically to a carpenter, but rather a skilled artisan who would as likely work with stone as with wood.

He knew. He knew when he came to town how it would go. And that last stinging rebuke that even in his own home he was without true honor, well, that was too much for his brothers and sisters. Even they took offense, though I tried to tell them he was not rejecting us. But it certainly felt that way, on that day. But just as bad was what a member of the town said—they called him "The son of Miriam." Now you might think that was a proper and honorable thing to do, but in fact it isn't. Even if the father is deceased a son is still called "The son of his father." No, this snide remark was suggesting something inappropriate about Yeshua's origins—he was only the "Son of Miriam," and by implication, not of Joseph, of blessed memory.

I suppose since we are telling all the bad news, we may as well go to the day that a sword did indeed pierce my own heart, as Simeon had long ago suggested would happen. Here is how the story was told here in Ephesus.

"Near the cross of Yeshua stood his mother, his mother's sister, Miriam the wife of Clopas, and Miriam of Migdal. When Yeshua saw his mother there, and the disciple whom he loved standing nearby, he said to her, 'Woman, here is your son,' and to the disciple, 'Here is your mother.' From time on, this disciple took her into his home." [John 19]

None of the Twelve were there at the cross. They had all run away. None of Yeshua's siblings were at the cross, nor did they fulfill the duty of burying their kin when Yeshua died. They were too humiliated. They felt Yeshua had brought extreme shame on his whole family. I alone held out hope this was not so. So I was there to the bitter end. I saw it all, though no mother should have to see the death of her precious child, and especially not in this hideous fashion. Crucifixion was indeed the most shameful way to die in our time and world, and if Yeshua had not risen from the dead, vindicated by G-d himself, there would have been no recovery of honor, rather only shame for us to live with forever. People believed that how a person dies most reveals their character, and what were people to think of Yeshua if he died a death reserved for revolutionaries or slaves? Horrible, horrible things is what they would think, and rightly so. We Jews even had a saying based in our Torah—"Cursed be he who hangs upon a tree." How could Yeshua be God's blessed or anointed one, and yet he died this way? It made no sense to any of us, not even me at the time.

I was not really prepared for Yeshua's last will and testament, handing me over to Eliezar. I did not realize that Yeshua wanted me to stay in the vicinity of Jerusalem, because he knew there would soon be a family reunion of sorts! Once he arose, he told the Eleven to stay in Jerusalem until they were empowered by God's Spirit. So it was that I stayed in Bethany, and then was part of the praying disciples in the upper room, with Yeshua's brothers after he arose, and before Pentecost [see Acts 1:14]. If you want to know what happened after that, after Yeshua returned to the Father, I went with the Beloved Disciple to Ephesus, and spent the rest of my life and ministry there. In the end, my trust in my son was rewarded, and indeed the good news about him has been spreading from Jerusalem to Roma. I am thankful to have become a spiritual mother to many since those days in Jerusalem, to be a part of offering salvation to all, from the least, the last, and the lost, to the most, the first, and the found.

CHAPTER NINETEEN

PONTIUS PILATE

I SHOULD HAVE LISTENED TO MY WIFE. SHE HAD NIGHTMARES ABOUT THAT man. I should have had nothing to do with him.[1] Had I listened, I might not be in exile as I am now, in Vienne. I was recalled by Tiberius about seven years after the death of "The King of the Jews" because I handled a later Samaritan uprising too brutally. What happened of course was the Jews reported me to the emperor for the handling of the Yeshua debacle, and then the Samaritans did likewise later, and that was the end of my being the prefect over Judea. But you will not be interested in the recriminations and regrets now. You want to know the official Roman record as to what exactly led to the death of Yeshua. Actually the report given in Ephesus by one of Yeshua's disciples who was an eyewitness to all these things is quite

1. For those wanting more direct evidence about Pilate, see my *New Testament History: A Narrative Account* (Baker, 2003).

accurate, so for sake of convenience I will point you to it. I later obtained a copy of it . . .

"*Then the Jewish leaders took Yeshua from Caiaphas to the palace of the Roman governor. By now it was early morning, and to avoid ceremonial uncleanness they did not enter the palace, because they wanted to be able to eat the Passover. So Pilate came out to them and asked, 'What charges are you bringing against this man?'*

"*'If he were not a criminal,' they replied, 'we would not have handed him over to you.'*

"*Pilate said, 'Take him yourselves and judge him by your own law.'*

"*'But we have no right to execute anyone,' they objected. This took place to fulfill what Yeshua had said about the kind of death he was going to die.*

"*Pilate then went back inside the palace, summoned Yeshua and asked him, 'Are you the king of the Jews?'*

"*'Is that your own idea,' Yeshua asked, 'or did others talk to you about me?'*

"*'Am I a Jew?' Pilate replied. 'Your own people and chief priests handed you over to me. What is it you have done?'*

"*Yeshua said, 'My kingdom is not of this world. If it were, my servants would fight to prevent my arrest by the Jewish leaders. But now my kingdom is from another place.'*

"*'You are a king, then!' said Pilate.*

"*Yeshua answered, 'You say that I am a king. In fact, the reason I was born and came into the world is to testify to the truth. Everyone on the side of truth listens to me.'*

"*'What is truth?' retorted Pilate. With this he went out again to the Jews gathered there and said, 'I find no basis for a charge against him. But it is your custom for me to release to you one prisoner at the time of the Passover. Do you want me to release 'the king of the Jews'?'*

"*They shouted back, 'No, not him! Give us Barabbas!' Now Barabbas had taken part in an uprising.*

"*Then Pilate took Yeshua and had him flogged. The soldiers twisted together a crown of thorns and put it on his head. They clothed him in a purple robe and went up to him again and again, saying, 'Hail, king of the Jews!' And they slapped him in the face.*

"*Once more Pilate came out and said to the Jews gathered there, 'Look, I am bringing him out to you to let you know that I find no basis for a charge against him.'*

"*When Yeshua came out wearing the crown of thorns and the purple robe, Pilate said to them, 'Here is the man!'*

"*As soon as the chief priests and their officials saw him, they shouted, 'Crucify! Crucify!'*

"*But Pilate answered, 'You take him and crucify him. As for me, I find no basis for a charge against him.'*

"*The Jewish leaders insisted, 'We have a law, and according to that law he must die, because he claimed to be the Son of God.'*

"*When Pilate heard this, he was even more afraid, and he went back inside the palace. 'Where do you come from?' he asked Yeshua, but Yeshua gave him no answer.*

"*'Do you refuse to speak to me?' Pilate said. 'Don't you realize I have power either to free you or to crucify you?'*

"*Yeshua answered, 'You would have no power over me if it were not given to you from above. Therefore the one who handed me over to you is guilty of a greater sin.'*

"*From then on, Pilate tried to set Yeshua free, but the Jewish leaders kept shouting, 'If you let this man go, you are no friend of Caesar. Anyone who claims to be a king opposes Caesar.'*

"*When Pilate heard this, he brought Yeshua out and sat down on the judge's seat at a place known as the Stone Pavement (which in Aramaic is Gabbatha). It was the day of Preparation of the Passover; it was about noon.*

"*'Here is your king,' Pilate said to the Jews.*

"*But they shouted, 'Take him away! Take him away! Crucify him!'*

"*'Shall I crucify your king?' Pilate asked.*

"*'We have no king but Caesar,' the chief priests answered.*

"*Finally Pilate handed him over to them to be crucified.*" [John 18–19]

This is a surprisingly fair account of exactly what happened. Let me be clear that I do not like Jews, and liked even less scheming Jewish officials trying to manipulate me. I decided I would try to do my best *not* to give them what they wanted because I was suspicious that they simply wanted to get rid of Yeshua because he was seen as a threat to their power and authority. The longer the judicial process went, however, the more afraid I became that Yeshua might indeed be more dangerous than even Barabbas, who was indeed a zealot, a revolutionary.

Understand that Yeshua was being judged by Roman law, not Jewish law. We did not allow the Jews the right of capital punishment. We reserved that right to ourselves since Judea was now a Roman province. But there were really only two main crimes for which someone could be found guilty of a capital crime and receive the "extreme" punishment, as it was called—crucifixion. One was leading a slave revolt or being a runaway slave, which is why crucifixion was called the slave's punishment. The other was *majestatis*—that is treason. Claiming to be a ruler in a region that was a Roman province, if you were neither a Roman prefect nor a client king appointed or approved by Rome, constituted treason. Was Yeshua actually making such a claim? Was he claiming rulership over Judea, and so usurping the rights of the emperor, and indeed my own subordinate role? I did not really think so, and when I heard he was actually from Galilee, I sent him off to Herod Antipas who was in town for the festival. But Herod simply sent him back to me and did nothing!

It was hard to tell about Yeshua. On the one hand, he kept asking me questions like "Is this king idea coming from you or did someone put you up to it?" And then on top of that, he kept saying, "My realm is not of this world," of which I could make no sense. I tried to simply have the man flogged and released, but the crowds whipped up by the Jewish authorities were not having it. I had no desire to release a real criminal like Barabbas, but the real tipping point was when the threat came "If you don't do this, you are no friend of Caesar." Somebody knew what *amicus Caesaris* meant to me. Being a "friend of Caesar" meant you were on the emperor's good side, on his good list, showed promise, and might look for promotion to a better province. But if you were the subject of constant complaints from your subjects, complaints an embassy would take to the Emperor Tiberius on Capri, well then you could kiss goodbye your climb up the ladder of success, the *cursus honorum* as we Romans call it. And eventually, that was exactly what happened. I got sent into exile by Tiberius due to a later matter involving those cursed Samaritans. Still to this day I am not sure whether Yeshua was just toying with me, or was really claiming to be some sort of king.

Even though I finally gave in and handed Yeshua over for execution, I was adamant about the *titulus*, the placard on the cross labeling the man's crimes. I insisted it read, "Yeshua of Nazareth, King of the Jews" because I just knew those Jewish authorities would gnash their teeth over that. That was the only thing that left me with a smile on my face about this whole sordid affair. I washed my hands of the matter, but it still haunts my mind.

History is full of ironies. I have no future, being here in Gaul in exile. Meanwhile, I keep hearing about the spreading of the proclamation of

Yeshua as a rival to the emperor, indeed as a savior to all humankind. I suppose it's a case of he must increase and I must decrease. It's funny how fate works.

CHAPTER TWENTY

THE MOTHER OF JOHN MARK

I LIVED IN JERUSALEM WITH MY SON, JOHN MARK. HE WAS YOUNG, ONLY A teenager during the time of Yeshua's ministry. He did not become a disciple then, though, yes, it is true he was the boy who ran off leaving his outer garment behind on the Mount of Olives. He was there when Yeshua was taken captive by the temple authorities and the Romans working with them. We both became disciples of Yeshua after the fact, after he appeared as the risen one to various people, including our friends Peter and John. We became part of the Jerusalem community of the Way, meeting with other disciples of Yeshua in Solomon's Portico in the temple precincts, and in homes as well, including in my home. I was honored to provide one of the venues where the earliest followers of Yeshua might safely meet. My husband had been a person of some means, and he had left the house to Mark and myself. I only have time to tell you one story about those meetings in our house, and it is a humorous one, now that I look back on it. Here's the tale itself, as told later by Luke . . .

"It was about this time that King Herod arrested some who belonged to the church, intending to persecute them. He had Jacob, the brother of John, put to death with the sword. When he saw that this met with approval among the Jews, he proceeded to seize Peter also. This happened during the Festival of Unleavened Bread. After arresting him, he put him in prison, handing him over to be guarded by four squads of four soldiers each. Herod intended to bring him out for public trial after the Passover.

"So Peter was kept in prison, but the church was earnestly praying to G-d for him.

"The night before Herod was to bring him to trial, Peter was sleeping between two soldiers, bound with two chains, and sentries stood guard at the entrance. Suddenly an angel of the Lord appeared and a light shone in the cell. He struck Peter on the side and woke him up. 'Quick, get up!' he said, and the chains fell off Peter's wrists.

"Then the angel said to him, 'Put on your clothes and sandals.' And Peter did so. 'Wrap your cloak around you and follow me,' the angel told him. Peter followed him out of the prison, but he had no idea that what the angel was doing was really happening; he thought he was seeing a vision. They passed the first and second guards and came to the iron gate leading to the city. It opened for them by itself, and they went through it. When they had walked the length of one street, suddenly the angel left him.

"Then Peter came to himself and said, 'Now I know without a doubt that the Lord has sent his angel and rescued me from Herod's clutches and from everything the Jewish people were hoping would happen.'

"When this had dawned on him, he went to the house of Miriam the mother of John, also called Mark, where many people had gathered and were praying. Peter knocked at the outer entrance, and a servant named Rhoda came to answer the door. When she recognized Peter's voice, she was so overjoyed she ran back without opening it and exclaimed, 'Peter is at the door!'

"'You're out of your mind,' they told her. When she kept insisting that it was so, they said, 'It must be his angel.'

"But Peter kept on knocking, and when they opened the door and saw him, they were astonished. Peter motioned with his hand for them to be quiet and described how the Lord had brought him out of prison. 'Tell Jacob and the other brothers and sisters about this,' he said, and then he left for another place.

"In the morning, there was no small commotion among the soldiers as to what had become of Peter. After Herod had a thorough search made for him and did not find him, he cross-examined the guards and ordered that they be executed." [Acts 12]

You have to admit, the image of Peter himself banging and banging on the door, and no one is letting him in, and poor Rhoda being accused of having seen a ghost, produces a smile, as does the whole picture of bleary-eyed Peter stumbling out of jail assuming he was having a vision of an angel, when actually he was being rescued! Anyway, finally it dawned on us that someone must be doing the banging, and Peter was finally let in. In fact, this was the last time in Luke's chronicle that Peter was ever in Jerusalem, except for the Jerusalem council, which happened in mid-century. The story related above is entirely true and it transpired in the tumultuous period about ten years or so after Yeshua's death when Herod Agrippa was throwing his weight around, and trying to gain more honor and status by persecuting the followers of Yeshua. Eventually, of course, G-d called him to account, as Luke's story goes on to relate.

A couple of more important things should be mentioned about this story. We continued to stay and make a witness in Jerusalem despite the persecutions. We believed the Lord was with us in those dark days. Secondly, notice that Jacob, the brother of Yeshua himself was now head of the Jerusalem church, after Peter had begun to travel and evangelize Jews, and leaders such as Jacob son of Zebedee had been martyred. We knew from the promise of Yeshua that his assembly, his community would not die out. But it became more and more difficult to bear witness without reprisals in Jerusalem. I was just thankful I could play hostess to a household meeting where we worshiped and prayed, and wept and learned and ate together.

CHAPTER TWENTY-ONE

THE CENTURION

My name is Gaius Julius Africanus. I serve in the Legio Ferrata, the so-called "Ironclad," the sixth legion of the emperor. We have a long and storied past. It was my legion that helped build the massive aqueduct at Caesarea Maritima bringing fresh water down from the northern hills, not to mention building the Hippodrome there as well. We have served in this land first as troops that helped Herod the Great maintain control of the land, and then under our Roman governors when Judea became a new province of Rome after the time of Archelaeus, the unfortunate son of Herod who couldn't even manage to rule a small territory like Judea. My father, who served under Julius Caesar, would have laughed about that. The Jews may be contentious, but they are hardly the Gauls, or Hannibal's people.

As centurions, we have many duties, but our main tasks are peace-keeping ones at this point—stopping squabbles between Judeans and Samaritans, or between foreigners and Jews, maintaining order during those numerous Jewish religious festivals in Jerusalem, putting down riots or insurrections over taxes and other things, collecting taxes and supervising the census when it comes time to do a new one. All in all, it's not bad work, and it's certainly not boring, but frankly, I'm tired of it and my plan is to muster out soon. I've been granted a plot of land near the governor's headquarters in Caesarea, and it's a nice piece of land with a seaside view. I could do worse. My son Cornelius is already there. He's served for the last four years in this same legion. I am quite proud of him. But his enthusiasm for military service is even less than mine at this point, and I partly attribute this to his becoming enamored with the Jewish religion.

At first I scoffed at the notion that there was only one god, though I have to admit, it makes religious duties a lot simpler. You know who's likely to judge you or bring benefit and blessing to you. You don't have to guess or consult an oracle to figure it out. Lately, Cornelius has really surprised me in that he has been contacting the followers of a prophet named Yeshua, and in particular someone with the nickname of "Rock." I'd like to see him, see what kind of human specimen he is. This actually shocked me, because Cornelius knows perfectly well that I was one of the centurions who watched the man die outside the city walls in Jerusalem, and actually I'm the one who won the throw of the dice with a Venus throw, and so procured his seamless cloak. It's a beautiful piece of weaving, and I still have it. Maybe I should give it to Cornelius, since he seems bound and determined to become a follower of Yeshua. How very odd that seems to me. Crucified men don't usually continue to have a following after their execution, let me tell you. But this man was different, strangely different, and it was hard to put one's finger on why, exactly. Since you've got some time, let me take you back to that Passover now more than ten years ago in Jerusalem.

First of all, you need to realize that Passover is the biggest festival. I would reckon sometimes a half million people show up in a town a tenth of that size normally. To say the least, this makes a prefect nervous, so the legions go down to Jerusalem from Caesarea to make sure nothing erupts. Pontius Pilate does not brook anything that looks like trouble. He wants it snuffed out and dealt with quickly. He is a hard man, even a brutal man, and oh yes, he despises Jews. If you ask me, he's the wrong man for the job here, but don't tell anyone I said so.

Now normally, normally, you don't want to do any trials or executions during festival time. That's supposed to be a time of religious celebration, and no mistake. Neither our Roman authorities, nor even the Jewish authorities want anything like that happening during what they call Passover. If you ask me it's a strange festival—they claim they were liberated from Egypt by plagues of bugs, and frogs, and blood. Just weird. Anyway, at this Passover we were on heightened alert because the word was out that Yeshua and his entourage were coming to town, and sure enough he rode into town like a king, on a donkey, with loud praises echoing down the main road into the Joppa Gate, and then on top of that, he went into the temple and turned over some tables and some animal cages and made the money changers and the sellers of sacrificial animals unbelievably mad. This was not good. I was not surprised when later in the week we got the call from the high priest, Caiaphas to bring a cohort and help take this man prisoner. He seemed dangerous.

Now I was on duty on that occasion, and I have to say it was strange. Yeshua had exactly two disciples who had short swords, which was hardly going to win them any battles against us, and the one called Rock actually cut off the high priest's servants ear. I was standing right there when it happened, and then even more strange, I saw Yeshua pick up the ear, and heal the man's head on the spot! That spooked me and the boys, I can tell you. I had never seen anything like that at all.

So we carted Yeshua off to Caiaphas's house, thinking we were done with our duty. Well, I should have realized a soldier's duty is never done. The next morning Pilate calls on us, after a trial at the Pavement near Herod's palace, to take Yeshua off and execute him. He was a sorry sight. He had been flogged, though not severely, but he was beaten up enough that he could hardly carry the cross piece to the point of execution. We finally had to force a man from Cyrene to carry it the rest of the way.

I noticed that the placard, which was hanging around Yeshua's neck temporarily until we got to the crucifixion spot at Golgotha, said "Yeshua of Nazareth, King of the Jews" in Latin, Greek, and some Jewish language I couldn't read. This seemed like a sad parody to me, or at least a poke in the eye to the high priest who wanted it to read "This man claims to be . . ." But Pilate was adamant. He wouldn't change what was written. He had the bit between his teeth and was determined not to give the high priest everything he wanted. I did notice however that Pilate seemed nervous. He wanted this whole thing over with quickly, as did the Jewish authorities.

So we got to Golgotha, and nailed Yeshua to the cross piece, and then to the footplate, and hauled up the cross with ropes and pulleys. He was crucified between two revolutionaries whom Pilate had been holding. Cornelius found an account of this whole affair written by some follower of Yeshua, and it's pretty accurate so I'll let you read it now . . .

"As the soldiers led him away, they seized Simon from Cyrene, who was on his way in from the country, and put the cross on him and made him carry it behind Yeshua. A large number of people followed him, including women who mourned and wailed for him. Yeshua turned and said to them, 'Daughters of Jerusalem, do not weep for me; weep for yourselves and for your children. For the time will come when you will say, "Blessed are the childless women, the wombs that never bore and the breasts that never nursed!" Then

they will say to the mountains, "Fall on us!"

and to the hills, "Cover us!"

For if people do these things when the tree is green, what will happen when it is dry?'

"Two other men, both criminals, were also led out with him to be executed. When they came to the place called the Skull, they crucified him there, along with the criminals—one on his right, the other on his left. Yeshua said, 'Father, forgive them, for they do not know what they are doing.' And they divided up his clothes by casting lots.

"The people stood watching, and the rulers even sneered at him. They said, 'He saved others; let him save himself if he is G-d's Messiah, the Chosen One.'

"The soldiers also came up and mocked him. They offered him wine vinegar and said, 'If you are the king of the Jews, save yourself.'

"There was a written notice above him, which read: THIS IS THE KING OF THE JEWS.

"One of the criminals who hung there hurled insults at him: 'Aren't you the Messiah? Save yourself and us!'

"But the other criminal rebuked him. 'Don't you fear G-d,' he said, 'since you are under the same sentence? We are punished justly, for we are getting what our deeds deserve. But this man has done nothing wrong.'

"Then he said, 'Yeshua, remember me when you come into your kingdom.'

"Yeshua answered him, 'Truly I tell you, today you will be with me in paradise.'

"It was now about noon, and darkness came over the whole land until three in the afternoon, for the sun stopped shining. And the curtain of the *temple was torn in two. Yeshua called out with a loud voice, 'Father, into your hands I commit my spirit.' When he had said this, he breathed his last.*

"*The centurion, seeing what had happened, praised G-d and said, 'Surely this was a righteous man.' When all the people who had gathered to witness this sight saw what took place, they beat their breasts and went away. But all those who knew him, including the women who had followed him from Galilee, stood at a distance, watching these things.*" [Luke 23]

Yes, it was me who made the exclamation at the end of things. The death of Yeshua was so different from the death of criminals who usually are cursing some G-d and ranting and raving against their tormentors until the very end. I had never ever heard of someone forgiving or asking the gods to forgive their executioners! Never. Nor had I ever heard of someone offering 'paradise' (which I presume means Elysium)[1] to a criminal dying on a cross. There were so many things about this death that were extraordinary. Yes, he had spoken of his sense of being G-d forsaken at one point, but that's normal. What is not normal is thinking that after crucifixion you are going to Elysium or Paradise! Listening to all he said from the cross, and how he treated even those who berated and abused him, I concluded there must be something special about him. He must be a righteous person, or in some way a son of the gods, because mere guilty mortals don't die like that. They don't die commending their souls to the deity. If anything they either curse the deity or express the feeling that they've been cursed and doomed by the deity. Not this man. He was different, and so I saw something noble in him, something righteous, and kind, and forgiving. That's why I said what I did.

Now later, I was not on the tomb watch duty, though some of my unit drew that assignment. I heard about the bizarre circumstance that the tomb turned out to be empty despite the fact that the guards were there the whole time. How exactly that happened, when there was a big stone rolled in front of the tomb, remains a mystery, but my son Cornelius says it was an act of some divine being, an angel maybe, that released him from his grave. The story is that he rose from the dead. Now me, I find that hard to swallow. We Romans don't believe in that peculiar form of afterlife that some Jews affirm. We believe in the immortal soul, so I could accept the notion that perhaps his soul was rescued from Hades at most. But, where then did the body go? Was there an apotheosis—was he taken up into the divine realm? There was that story about him as well. Cornelius says *both things*

1. Elysium was the positive afterlife the Romans spoke of, for the blessed few.

happened. He both rose in the flesh, and then ascended. I don't understand it. Why would one need a body in the afterlife? In any case, I hope to get some more answers tomorrow.

Tomorrow, I've been invited to some sort of religious water ritual. My son is being baptized by this man nicknamed Rock. I intend to ask some questions. And I've decided I'm giving Yeshua's cloak to my son as a present in light of his new commitment to the man. It seems only fitting, not least because I have no real need of it or use for it. Only two more weeks before I muster out, and it's time for me to settle accounts anyway, and get rid of things I don't need to keep. I'm an old soldier in a young man's job, and it's time to move on. When I saw Yeshua die, I said a little prayer of praise for getting to meet such a noble soul. Maybe soon I will understand him better. Even tough old soldiers need divine assistance once in a while.

CHAPTER TWENTY-TWO

JOANNA

YOU MAY THINK YOU KNOW MY STORY, BUT PROBABLY NOT ALL OF IT. YES, I was one of the original disciples of Yeshua in Galilee. I was a high-born woman, who had married Chuza, who rose to the lofty position of being Herod Antipas's estate agent. Chuza managed the estates of Herod all over Galilee. Occasionally, I traveled with him, and it was in those travels that I first encountered Yeshua. He was exorcizing a demon out of a woman who was writhing on the ground and foaming at the mouth. I will never forget that dramatic scene. And when the woman sat up, bathed in sweat, but in her right mind, and asked Yeshua for some water, I knew I was in the presence of someone extraordinary.

Despite Chuza's opposition I became one of the traveling disciples of Yeshua. He warned me not to do it. Warned me it could cost him his job. Warned me at the end that he would have to divorce me to keep his job, and

106

when I still persisted in following Yeshua, the next time I came home, he handed me the writ of divorce. This was right after John the Baptizer was beheaded, and Herod was perturbed about Yeshua being John come back from the dead to haunt him. He had given Chuza an ultimatum to either get rid of his wife who supported Yeshua, or be thrown out on the road with no source of income. He chose the job.

Yes, I was one of Yeshua's patrons, so to speak, providing provisions for the disciples as they traveled, and traveling funds as well. I had come into the marriage with Chuza with a considerable dowry, which I kept after the divorce. It was a good thing I did too, as it was needed, as there were times when Yeshua and his followers could not rely on the system of standing hospitality in villages in Galilee and Judea. Some people who had heard the reports about Yeshua closed their doors when we came to town, even when we went to Nazareth, Chorazim, and other places near his home.

For the most part, people had a hard time knowing what to make of Yeshua. On the one hand, they wanted and needed the healings and help. On the other hand his teaching and his radical discipleship demands were simply too much for some people to accept. He was asking for a radical commitment, which he characterized using the dramatic metaphor of carrying a cross. Each one was to take up a cross and follow him. I took this to mean that one had committed one's very life, and was sacrificing everything to follow him. That's exactly what I did, letting my husband go without an argument. He had not been a bad husband, but if it was a choice between him and following Yeshua, that in my mind was no choice. Fortunately, Chuza made it easy for me by choosing before I had to do so.

It was seen by many in Galilee as scandalous that a bunch of women who were neither the relatives of Yeshua, nor of any of the Twelve, were wandering around the country helping him proclaim the good news. You can bet that was the subject of much gossip, to say the least. They said things like "What kind of prophet does this? What kind of prophet even dines with sinners and tax collectors?" There were many controversial aspects to Yeshua's ministry. His teaching gave women permission to remain single for the sake of the coming of G-d's final Dominion, and so assume roles other than that of wife and mother. This was revolutionary.

And of course, lots of people could not understand why a well-born woman of some means like me would seek out Yeshua. I didn't need healing or sustenance. I didn't lack for the necessities of life. The feeding of the five thousand didn't have me as one of the recipients. I was constantly asked—'Why are you following Yeshua?" followed by 'Well-born women don't do these kinds of things, it's shameful especially when you don't need healing or help!' My response was—'he has G-d's words of life, to whom else should I go? He is bringing in G-d's final saving reign upon the earth, why wouldn't I want to be part of that joyful activity?' They usually just looked at me strangely after I said this, and walked off muttering.

Miriam of Migdal and I and the other women all traveled with Yeshua up to Jerusalem for that final fateful Passover. We saw it all—the triumphal entry, the cleansing of the temple, heard the predictions of the demise of Herod's temple in a generation, ate a final meal with him, watched his execution from a distance, went to the tomb Sunday morning to anoint the body, found the tomb empty and heard the angels say he was risen, told the male disciples, who just threw up their hands and called it a woman's fantasy. I actually saw the risen Yeshua on various occasions before he ascended.

You perhaps know all this already, but you do not know the rest of the story. So I will share it with you now. I joined the Jerusalem Jewish followers of Yeshua, determined to further his cause, and share in the proclaiming of the good news. In that context I met another man, a man who had a Roman name—Andronicus. He was a Jew from Rome, who had come for the Pentecost festival, and was present when Peter made his first great proclamation, with many people from all over the empire becoming followers of Yeshua. The Spirit fell on him, just as it fell on me and others during that time. Andronicus was unmarried, but actually had come to Jerusalem looking for a good Jewish woman to be his wife. We became close, and were married only a few months after Pentecost, with the aid of my friends in the Jerusalem community of Yeshua followers. I had not looked for a new spouse, had not expected such a thing, but sometimes the serendipity of G-d happens without human plans. We were a very happy couple, and resolved to work hard for the Lord, doing it together. I had no children, nor did he, and our work became our focus.

It was not long before the Jewish followers of Yeshua had become so numerous in Jerusalem, that we began to suffer persecution, prosecution, even execution. Jacob, son of Zebedee was martyred as was Stephen before him. And one of the leading agents of our misery was a man called Saul of Tarsus, who was determined to eradicate our sect. But then something unexpected happened. I had learned to expect the unexpected in the following of Yeshua, but even I did not see this coming—Saul while on the way from Jerusalem to Damascus to take more of our number captive and bring them to trial in Jeusalem, was suddenly struck blind by the heavenly Yeshua himself! That's what I call real divine intervention, which of course we had prayed for, but never expected in this form. So it was that our enemy became our friend, our persecutor became our advocate, our pursuer became one of our leaders, though many of us were wary of him for a long time. He went off to Arabia and also his native region of Cilicia for a long time before returning to Jerusalem. But when he did, and he received the right hand of fellowship from Jacob, Yeshua's brother, and from Peter and John, it was at that juncture we decided G-d wanted us to be his helpers. We would go with him throughout the empire leading pagans to faith in Yeshua. That became our whole and sole mission, and it was difficult but thrilling work.

We were thrown in jail with Saul, who changed his name to Paul, we planted churches with Paul where none had existed before, we risked our necks for Paul, again and again. Believers began calling us all "the sent ones"—"apostles" if you will. Yes, I was the first female apostle. The criteria was simple: 1) having seen the risen Yeshua, and 2) having been gifted by the Spirit for evangelism. When we were in Roman contexts, I assumed the Roman form of my name—Junia, being the Latin equivalent of Joanna. We had many adventures, and misadventures too with Paul.

Eventually, we ended up in Roma, after the death of the Emperor Claudius when Jews were streaming back to the capital city, after many native Jews had been sent into exile by Claudius. After some years there of work, we had been apart from Paul for a good while and not heard from him. He had always planned to come to Roma, but he kept having things get in the way, and other duties prevent his coming. Finally we got a letter, carried by Phoebe from Corinth. She was his vanguard. He was coming thereafter. Here is portion of that letter he wrote to us in Roma . . .

Greet with every show of affection Andronicus and Junia, my fellow Jews who have been in prison with me. They are outstanding among the apostles, and they were in Christ before I was. [Romans 16]

At last we had heard from our fellow apostle. At last. But now we hear he may not ever make it to Roma—he is incarcerated in Caesarea Maritima, the very city I was born in! He is awaiting trial by the governor. There had been a riot in Jerusalem when he was in the Temple precincts, apparently with Titus, another coworker, and someone thought he had taken a pagan into the Jewish court. But he would never do that! So our hopes have been crushed once again. But knowing Paul, he will figure out a way to get to

Roma. He's a Roman citizen after all, and he has the law on his side when such unfortunate things happen. We are all dedicating a lot of prayer for his release, and arrival in Roma. My life has had many blessings, and working with both Yeshua and Paul, and my husband I count as the three biggest ones. But I suspect, G-d is not done with me yet. There is still much to be accomplished here, for example the binding together of the Jewish and gentile followers of Yeshua, who basically meet separately and are independent groups. Just because God's saving activity is happening does not mean all our problems and differences are instantly forgotten. So I ask you to pray for us as well, and I say grace and peace to you from our Lord and Savior, Yeshua, the Messiah.

CHAPTER TWENTY-THREE

THOMAS DIDYMUS

In case you are wondering, Yeshua chose twelve of us for a special role—to seek out and save the lost sheep of Israel, and on the judgment day to sit on twelve thrones, judging the twelve tribes, like in the days of old, the time of the judges. Perhaps your memory is a little foggy, but here's a list:—"These are the Twelve he appointed: Simon (to whom he gave the name Peter), Jacob son of Zebedee and his brother John (to them he gave the name Boanerges, which means 'sons of thunder'), Andrew, Philip, Bartholomew, Matthew, Thomas, James son of Alphaeus, Thaddaeus, Simon the Zealot and Judas Iscariot, who betrayed him" [Mark 3]. You'll find me there in the middle of the list. I was not in the inner circle of the Three, nor did I go and betray Yeshua like Judas. But I was one of the original Twelve chosen by Yeshua.

Somehow, as time has gone on, I've gotten a nickname—"Doubting Thomas"—but that's all wrong. I didn't merely have doubts, I disbelieved the stories about Yeshua rising from the dead. I had always had a sort of skeptical temperament anyway, and there came a day when I became a disbeliever! *Apistos* in Greek doesn't refer to doubt, it refers to unbelief! Now that we've gotten that straight, you'll better understand the most famous story told about me, where I re-embraced my faith in Yeshua, and saw him as much more than even a messiah or a prophet. Here's the story as Eliezar tells it . . .

"*Now Thomas (also known as Didymus), one of the Twelve, was not with the disciples when Yeshua came. So the other disciples told him, 'We have seen the Lord!'*

"*But he said to them, 'Unless I see the nail marks in his hands and put my finger where the nails were, and put my hand into his side, I will not believe.'*

"*A week later his disciples were in the house again, and Thomas was with them. Though the doors were locked, Yeshua came and stood among them and said, 'Peace be with you!' Then he said to Thomas, 'Put your finger here; see my hands. Reach out your hand and put it into my side. Stop disbelieving and believe!'*

"*Thomas said to him, 'My Lord and my G-d!'*

"*Then Yeshua told him, 'Because you have seen me, you have believed; blessed are those who have not seen and yet have believed.'*" [John 20]

To fully understand this climax in my life story, you need to know some of the backstory. First of all, I am called Didymus because I have a twin brother. He was also a member of Yeshua's disciples, he's Matthew, with whom I am regularly grouped in the lists of the Twelve. The nickname stuck with me. Yeshua seems to have liked nicknames, some of which he coined himself like "Boanerges" and "Cephas." I was not a tax collector like my brother, but I had some of the same skeptical demeanor he had. For example, at one point Yeshua decided to go back to Judea and help the family of Miriam and Martha who had a sick brother, and this was after people had already tried to do away with Yeshua in Jerusalem. This prompted me to say to the rest of the disciples, "Let us also go, that we may die with him." This was not sarcasm, but rather reflects my rather fatalistic view of things at the time.

Perhaps you have also come across another mention of me from during the period of the last week of Yeshua's life. During one evening's teaching, I interrupted what Yeshua was saying, when he confidently asserted that by now we surely knew where he was going.

To this I retorted, "Lord, we don't know where you are going, so how can we know the way?" Yeshua answered, "I am the way and the truth and the life. No one comes to the Father except through me. If you really know me, you will know my Father as well. From now on, you do know him and have seen him."

I think you can tell something about my turn of mind, my bent, as it were. I was having more and more trouble trusting what Yeshua was saying, and then when he was crucified, I abandoned hope altogether. I was not doubting, I was disbelieving. So when the other disciples told me he had appeared to them in the upper room where we met, I scoffed. I told them, I would need to not merely see him, but touch and feel his wounds to be sure it was the same man.

The interesting thing was, a week later after he first appeared, I had agreed to take one more meal with the remaining disciples before I headed back to Galilee to take up a different line of work, and then he appeared quite personally to me, even me, disbelieving me. Perhaps you noticed from the quoting of the story above that actually I never did touch his healed wounds. He was so palpably real, I was so close I could even feel his breath, that I had no need to. My disbelief vanished in an instant, and I made a profession of faith in him that has since become something of a standard. He is both our Lord, and our G-d, not as a displacement of the Father, Abba, but as his only begotten Son, another personal expression of the one G-d. Yeshua reminded us all that believing leads to seeing, but in my case seeing was required for believing, so weak was my capacity for faith in Yeshua at the time.

You may have wondered what has happened to me since then? At first I went and shared the news about Yeshua with those in the province of Syria. This went well enough in Damascus and elsewhere, but once the churches were well established there, and since I was still in good health, I felt led to go further afield. I had heard the stories of Alexander going to the ends of the earth, and crossing into a land of rivers and elephants. This is not a land where Jews had ever been in exile, but I was attracted to go somewhere no follower of Yeshua had gone before. I am writing you now, from on board a ship sailing around Sheba. The captain says it will take many weeks to arrive in the land I am referring to. In the meantime, I would ask that you ponder my story. Remember, if Yeshua can even restore me to faith who had stopped believing in him, he can do this for others as well. Take heed to my example, and go and do otherwise than I did until that Sunday when he appeared to me. Yeshua said the strong faith is the one that doesn't need to see to believe. I've come to know that in any case, believing leads to seeing.[1]

1. There is a rather strong and early Christian tradition that Thomas was the first to evangelize in what came to be called India. See now Brian Shelton's *Quest for the Historical Apostles: Tracing their Lives and Legacies* (Baker, 2018) 173–86.

CHAPTER TWENTY-FOUR

MIRIAM OF MIGDAL

I AM THE DAUGHTER OF A MAN WHO RAN A PROFITABLE FISH FACTORY ON the northwest corner of the sea called Kinneret. We lived in the prosperous village of Migdal or Magdala, and we attended synagogue at the newest of the synagogues near the fish factory. All was well in my life until I got involved with Laban. Laban was a young man fascinated with the dark arts. He liked not only astrology but conjuring and dabbling with things that involved unclean spirits. I realize of course now it was the height of stupidity to get involved with something like that and become enmeshed in it, but I did, and then darkness closed in and took over my life. I was in my late teens, and suddenly I found myself shunned by my family and cast out of the synagogue. I lived in a cave at the bottom of the cliffs of Arbel, some distance from Magdala, but near to the main road from upper Galilee to the sea.

One day, when I was scrounging for berries, and stealing some milk from a goat that belonged to a neighboring goatherd, I looked up, and there was a man standing over me that caused my whole being to shudder. I thought at first he was going to try and abuse me, which had happened before, though I had fought the men off who tried it. But he said something odd—"Do you want to be well?"

Now I was, most of the time, so in thrall to the demons that I could not even speak for myself, but at that particular moment I found my voice and weakly said, "Yes." The next thing I knew I was screaming at the top of my lungs, rolling around in the dirt, and felt like someone had ripped my heart out! The man called Yeshua sent the demons in my life elsewhere, and I was free for the first time in several years. He sent me to the local priest to get acknowledgement that I was OK, so I could return to my village. I went to the mikveh first and got ritually clean, and put on my best clothes that I had left. Yet the priest would not receive me. Would not even let me into his doorway. He ran me off! Yeshua saw this happening and said "Don't be afraid, just come and follow me," and so I did.

I learned later I was the first woman to be a disciple of Yeshua, by which I mean a traveling disciple of his. This is why I am almost always listed first in the naming of the female disciples [see Luke 8:1–3]. I had never been a leader of anything before, but I found myself recruiting other women to follow Yeshua, so there would be less talk about Yeshua running around with a strange woman, a woman formerly demon possessed, and woman he was not kin to. Believe it or not, the first woman I had success in recruiting was a high-status woman named Joanna, who I met in Capernaum one day in the marketplace. She had come to buy fish, and no one was with her except a serving girl. I briefly told her who I was, and about the dramatic turn in my life, and she said immediately she wanted to meet this Yeshua. I said to her, "Come and see," and led her straight to Yeshua who was outside the synagogue in the village talking with some fishermen. Before long, there were some twenty or so men and women following Yeshua around, having become his disciples, in addition to which there were increasingly crowds clamoring for some help or healing.

Like Joanna, I was there when they crucified our *rabbouni*, our teacher, only I mustered up my courage and stood up close to the cross so I could hear what Yeshua was saying. His last words were precious to me, and to his mother and to others there. But my spirit was crushed when he gave up his spirit. All the hope, the anticipation of good things went out of my heart, and I began to grieve more deeply than I had ever done before, even when I lost my mother who died in childbearing when I was only seven. Still, I wanted to honor Yeshua, so we female disciples went to the tomb, saw where he was laid, and resolved to come back before dawn on the first day of the week to pay our last respects to Yeshua—bringing fresh linens and anointing oils and spices. The Beloved Disciple does a better job of telling the story from here, as I get too emotional when I remember what happened . . . Here is the account in his memoirs.

"Early on the first day of the week, while it was still dark, Miriam of Migdal went to the tomb and saw that the stone had been removed from the entrance. So she came running to Simon Peter and the other disciple, the one Yeshua loved, and said, 'They have taken the Lord out of the tomb, and we don't know where they have put him!'

"So Peter and the other disciple started for the tomb. Both were running, but the other disciple outran Peter and reached the tomb first. He bent over and looked in at the strips of linen lying there but did not go in. Then Simon Peter came along behind him and went straight into the tomb. He saw the strips of linen lying there, as well as the cloth that had been wrapped around Yeshua's head. The cloth was still lying in its place, separate from the linen. Finally the other disciple, who had reached the tomb first, also went inside. He saw and believed. (They still did not understand from Scripture that Yeshua had to rise from the dead.) Then the disciples went back to where they were staying.

"Now Miriam stood outside the tomb crying. As she wept, she bent over to look into the tomb and saw two angels in white, seated where Yeshua's body had been, one at the head and the other at the foot.

"They asked her, 'Woman, why are you crying?'

"'They have taken my Lord away,' she said, 'and I don't know where they have put him.' At this, she turned around and saw Yeshua standing there, but she did not realize that it was him.

"He asked her, 'Woman, why are you crying? Who is it you are looking for?'

"Thinking he was the gardener, she said, 'Sir, if you have carried him away, tell me where you have put him, and I will get him.'

"Yeshua said to her, 'Miriam.'

"She turned toward him and cried out in Aramaic, 'Rabboni!' (which means 'Teacher').

"Yeshua said, 'Do not hold on to me, for I have not yet ascended to the Father. Go instead to my brothers and tell them, "I am ascending to my Father and your Father, to my G-d and your God."'

"Miriam of Migdal went to the disciples with the news: 'I have seen the Lord!' And she told them that he had said these things to her." [John 20]

It is an extraordinary thing that Yeshua was not buried by his family members but only by his friends, in this case a secret disciple named Joseph. It was his tomb, and he was a wealthy man, so it was a nice garden tomb, fresh-cut, and never had there been a corpse in there thus far. There was no danger of mistaking Yeshua for some other body in that tomb. None whatsoever.

When we got to the tomb and it was both open and empty, after the initial shock I concluded the body must have been moved, or worse still stolen. Were we to be deprived of even the right to pay our last respects? It was a nightmare. I ran to tell Peter and Eliezar, and they came running and found it much as we had said, but they left none the wiser. Maybe they thought Yeshua had been taken up into heaven like Elijah, for Yeshua had talked several times about returning to the Father. I did not know what to think, but I was in any case inconsolable.

Now when I looked into the tomb again, after the men had left, I saw two bright ones, God's messengers. They were sitting at either end of the slab where the body of Yeshua had been laid. There was a void between them, but it was not devoid of meaning. They asked me an odd question—"Woman why are you crying?" It was odd because surely they knew why I was crying, and yet I gave a faltering answer. I was still deep in my grief, and even the appearance of angels could not change my mood.

Then I heard a voice outside the tomb say exactly the same thing, except in addition it asked: "Who are you looking for?" I should have paid closer attention to what he said—he called the object of my search *who*, not *what*. A mere corpse is just a *what*, not a *who*. Now I had not really looked at the source of the voice except to see a robed figure. I generally kept my eyes down or averted in the presence of a man anyway as that was respectful. For a moment I thought I was talking to the gardener, and asked where I could find and retrieve Yeshua's body, not thinking this was the task of at least two people. But then I hear my name. He called me by name—*Miriam*, and it sounded just like the first time he called my name near Magdala when I had returned to my right mind after the exorcism. I remembered

Yeshua saying that he was the good shepherd and he called his sheep by name, and they recognize the sound of his voice. I finally did!

I immediately went from grief to euphoria, shouted *"Rabbouni,"* and grabbed the hem of his garment and held on for dear life. He was alive, he was real, perhaps we could all be disciples once more! Yeshua had other plans. We were to go forward in a new direction, not merely continue what we had done before. In fact, he commissioned me, *me*, to go and tell the male disciples that he was risen and returning to his Father. I actually became the first person to proclaim "Yeshua is risen, he is risen indeed!"

I am sad to report that the men did not share my enthusiasm or even really believe what I told them. One of them, Thomas, called it a fantasy, a woman's fantasy. I was used to such derogatory remarks, but I paid it no mind. No one was going to steal my newfound joy, no one. Years later, I still get excited about that day, the day the whole world changed. Yeshua was raised from the dead, only now in a new body which was immune to disease, decay, and death, suffering, sin, and sorrow. A body we too at the resurrection will someday be privileged to have when we are remade in his image, the image of the risen Lord.

I have spent many years ever since sharing with women the good news about Yeshua, and it continues to spread, despite all attempts to squash it. Like a refreshing breeze it blows throughout the known world, bringing life with it. I say this message is unstoppable. If death could not put a stop to Yeshua and his ministry, then nothing can. No wonder he once said, "The gates of Hades will not prevail against my community." I will believe it until the day I die. I have remained here in Jerusalem with the believers here, but war is coming and many of our number have begun to leave. There was a prophecy that we should flee to Pella. Perhaps I will go, but whatever I do, and wherever I go, I know he will be with me. He walked through the valley of the shadow of death for us all, so I shall fear no evil. No one can take my joy or my Lord away from me again. He lives both in heaven and in me by the power of his Spirit whom he sent us. But perhaps I am telling you something you already know. If so, I thank you for listening to my story, and hope you may have one like it.

CHAPTER TWENTY FIVE

CLEOPAS

LET'S GET ONE THING STRAIGHT FROM THE START. MARY OF CLOPAS IS NOT
my wife. My name is Cleopas, not Clopas, but it is true that that day when
I was leaving Jerusalem, my wife and I were traveling together back to Emmaus, having attended the Passover festival. I had well and truly given up
on Yeshua being anyone special after that gruesome spectacle of a crucifixion. In my view G-d would never let that happen to his anointed one. It's
the ultimate form of public disgrace and humiliation—they are crucified in
the nude! The G-d we worship vindicates the righteous, he does not allow
them to be humiliated. Crucified messiah is a contradiction in terms if you
ask me, or at least . . . that's what I used to think. That's what I was thinking
as I started down the road to Emmaus. That was until a stranger came along
and journeyed with the two of us for a while. Here is the story as Luke tells
it . . .

"Now that same day two of them were going to a village called Emmaus, about seven miles from Jerusalem. They were talking with each other about everything that had happened. As they talked and discussed these things with each other, Yeshua himself came up and walked along with them; but they were kept from recognizing him.

"He asked them, 'What are you discussing together as you walk along?'

"They stood still, their faces downcast. One of them, named Cleopas, asked him, 'Are you the only one visiting Jerusalem who does not know the things that have happened there in these days?'

"'What things?' he asked.

"'About Yeshua of Nazareth,' they replied. 'He was a prophet, powerful in word and deed before G-d and all the people. The chief priests and our rulers handed him over to be sentenced to death, and they crucified him; but we had hoped that he was the one who was going to redeem Israel. And what is more, it is the third day since all this took place. In addition, some of our women amazed us. They went to the tomb early this morning but didn't find his body. They came and told us that they had seen a vision of angels, who said he was alive. Then some of our companions went to the tomb and found it just as the women had said, but Yeshua they did not see.'

"He said to them, 'How foolish you are, and how slow to believe all that the prophets have spoken! Did not the Messiah have to suffer these things and then enter his glory?' And beginning with Moses and all the Prophets, he explained to them what was said in all the Scriptures concerning himself.

"As they approached the village to which they were going, Yeshua continued on as if he were going farther. But they urged him strongly, 'Stay with us, for it is nearly evening; the day is almost over.' So he went in to stay with them.

"When he was at the table with them, he took bread, gave thanks, broke it and began to give it to them. Then their eyes were opened and they recognized him, and he disappeared from their sight. They asked each other, 'Were not our hearts burning within us while he talked with us on the road and opened the Scriptures to us?'

"They got up and returned at once to Jerusalem. There they found the Eleven and those with them, assembled together and saying, 'It is true! The Lord has risen and has appeared to Simon.' Then the two told what had happened on the way, and how Yeshua was recognized by them when he broke the bread." [Luke 24]

The story doesn't present me and my wife in a very flattering light, but it's sadly a true account. We really had given up, and were going home. End of story. As the story says, "We *had hoped* Yeshua was the one"—*hoped*, past tense. We had stopped hoping. A crucified messiah was not going to kick the Romans out and redeem Israel. Well . . . that's how I used to view it. It took a thorough review of those messianic prophetic texts, and even the texts from the law, by no less than Yeshua himself to change my mind. But of course, we did not know it was Yeshua at the time. We had seen him die, and we had not heard the reports of his being actually seen by one of the Twelve, only a report of some women who claimed to hear angels *saying* he was alive—but I dismissed that as the overheated imagination of some emotional women. Women's fantasies, is what I thought, but I was very wrong.

The Lord kept hammering home that the messiah must suffer. Must! The text that I found most persuasive was the suffering servant text in Isaiah, but I had always been taught that that was a reference to Israel, as a nation, suffering again and again, as G-d's witness in the world. After all, earlier in Isaiah we clearly hear the phrase "Israel my servant." I had never thought of applying that to G-d's anointed one as an individual. But this is precisely what I was being taught on the road to Emmaus.

One thing I would ask you to bear in mind is that as Judean followers of Yeshua, we only saw him when he came to town, and the venue in which we saw him was in homes, over the course of a meal. We heard about stories of the feeding of the 5,000, or healings by the sea of Galilee, or teachings in this or that synagogue, but Yeshua did none of that here in Jerusalem. So perhaps you will not be as surprised that we did not recognize the risen Yeshua until he broke bread with us. Then the light dawned. Mind you, when he was interpreting the Torah to us, our hearts lit up, with a new way of reading the Scriptures in regard to Messiah. But still, we didn't grasp that a man recently crucified was now having an intimate conversation with us.

And then with the shock of recognition during the sharing of bread, Yeshua suddenly just disappeared. I don't mean he walked out the door. I mean he suddenly was no longer sitting with us. One minute he is handing us some bread. The next minute no one is reclining on the couch across from us! Well that was just too much! I told my wife to throw on her outer garment, and we hiked back to Jerusalem that same night. By the time we got to the upper room, there was a buzz of conversation about Simon Peter having had a personal appearance of Yeshua, and we blurted out, "So did we!" There was now the testimony of several witnesses, and remember it is the witnesses of the male disciples that counted as legal witnesses. That's what was most convincing to us all. I must admit though, that I felt badly about doubting the initial testimony of the women who went to the tomb—Miriam, Joanna, and others. That was unfair. Perhaps the Lord was trying to teach us something in all of this. Miriam was the first one to see the risen Lord, then several other of the women as well. And Yeshua commissioned Miriam to come tell the men among us. It would appear that Yeshua has no problem with women teaching and proclaiming things even to men! That's just amazing, but then we knew Yeshua was a radical on some of these things.

The problem for me now is I have to rethink my whole concept of what "redeeming Israel" really looks like. Apparently it involves suffering rather than conquering, if Yeshua is the paradigm. Apparently it involves letting G-d vindicate us by his intervening judgment and redemption, instead of our trying to take vengeance and justice, and even stones, into our own hands. What was it Yeshua said about turning the other cheek, not returning violence for violence, and even loving our enemies, even the Samaritans and the Romans? As I say, I've got a lot of pondering and rethinking to do. Maybe G-d has a whole new way to redeem Israel. One of our number is a psalmist, and a poet, and he recently wrote a little song that begins this way—

> We were looking for a king,
> to slay our foes and lift us high.
> You came a little baby thing,
> That made a woman cry.[1]

If I've learned one thing from that tumultuous Passover season it is this—G-d doesn't answer our prayers and longings at the point of our request, but rather at the point of our need. He knew exactly what kind of messiah it would take to save the world. One that would die on a cross and offer a perfect atonement for sins. With benefit of hindsight, and an illumination of Scripture from Yeshua himself, I have realized that God's ways are not our ways, our eyes cannot see, the logic of love, nailed to a tree.

THE END

---

1. These are actually words written by C. S. Lewis's favorite poet and fantasy writer—George MacDonald.